THE FEEL THE FEAR GUIDE TO
LASTING LOVE
By Susan Jeffers, Ph.D.

Susan Jeffers has written another winner. This valuable book contains all the advice you will ever need for staying happily and deeply in love.

—JACK CANFIELD
Co-author of *Chicken Soup for the Couple's Soul®*
and author of *The Success Principles*

Susan Jeffers answers the age-old question, "What is love?" No matter the state of your relationship, you will be transformed by what you read.

—DEEPAK CHOPRA
Author of *The Book of Secrets, Ageless Body, Timeless Mind,*
The Seven Spiritual Laws of Success, Way of the Wizard,
and *Peace is the Way*

Susan Jeffers' new book is a great read. Her special zest, clarity and wisdom make the greatest love seem well within reach.

—MARIANNE WILLIAMSON
Author of *Everyday Grace, A Return to Love,*
and *The Gift of Change*

Susan Jeffers brings a rich new dimension to the understanding of what it means to love another person. Her wise insights will be an inspiration to you and a gift to your relationship.

—Barbara De Angelis, Ph.D.
Author of *What Women Want Men To Know*
and *How Did I Get Here?*

*When someday we say "I feel like Jeffers" rather than, "I feel like Cinderella," we will have a world of true love channeled through our higher purpose rather than a world of shattered dreams camouflaged by anti-depressants. Take the journey with **The Feel the Fear Guide to Lasting Love.***

—Warren Farrell, Ph.D.
Author of *Why Men Are the Way they Are*
and *Women Can't Hear What Men Don't Say*

The FEEL THE FEAR Guide to
LASTING LOVE

By Susan Jeffers, Ph.D.

(in alphabetical order)

Dare to Connect: Reaching Out in Romance, Friendship and the Workplace*

Embracing Uncertainty: Breakthrough Methods for Achieving Peace of Mind When Facing the Unknown*

End the Struggle and Dance with Life: How to Build Yourself Up When the World Gets You Down*

The Fear-Less Series
   *Inner Talk for a Confident Day**
   *Inner Talk for a Love that Works**
   *Inner Talk for Peace of Mind**

The Feel the Fear Series
   Feel the Fear ... and Beyond: Dynamic Techniques for Doing It Anyway*
   Feel the Fear and Do It Anyway: How to Turn Your Fear and Indecision into Confidence and Action*
   *The Feel the Fear Guide to Lasting Love**
   Feel the Fear Power Planner: 90 Days to a Fuller Life

I Can Handle It: Fifty Confidence Building Stories for Children 3 - 7 (co-authored with Donna Gradstein)

I'm Okay ... You're a Brat: Setting the Priorities Straight and Freeing You from the Guilt and Mad Myths of Parenthood* (Titled – Freeing Ourselves from the Mad Myths of Parenthood* in the UK)

Life is Huge! Laughing, Loving and Learning from it All

Losing a Love and Finding a Life: Healing the Pain of a Broken Relationship

Opening Our Hearts to Men: Transform Pain, Loneliness and Anger into Trust, Intimacy and Love*

The Little Book of Confidence

The Little Book of Peace of Mind

*Thoughts of Power and Love** (quotes from the works of Susan Jeffers)

* Also available in audiotape and/or CD

AUDIOTAPES FROM LIVE APPEARANCES
   The Art of Fearbusting (also available in CD)
   A Fearbusting Workshop
   Flirting from the Heart
   Opening Our Hearts to Each Other

www.susanjeffers.com

The FEEL THE FEAR Guide to

LASTING
LOVE

Susan Jeffers, Ph.D.

Jeffers
press

Published in the United States and Canada by Jeffers Press,
a division of Susan Jeffers, LLC,
P.O. Box 5338
Santa Monica, California 90409

www.jefferspress.com

Publisher's Cataloging-in-Publication
(Provided by Quality Books, Inc.)

Jeffers, Susan J.
   The feel the fear guide to-- lasting love / by Susan
Jeffers. -- 1st Jeffers Press ed.
   p. cm.
   Includes bibliographical references.
   ISBN 0-9745776-9-3

   1. Man-woman relationships. 2. Love. 3. Commitment
(Psychology) 4. Mate selection.   I. Title.

HQ801.J44 2005   306.7
                          QBI05-700143

ISBN 0-9745776-9-3

Printed in the USA

First Jeffers Press edition published 2005

Cover and text design by Dotti Albertine

To my wonderful husband,
Mark Shelmerdine

He fills my life with joy
and continues to teach me
so much about love.

He clearly is the inspiration
behind this book.

CONTENTS

ACKNOWLEDGMENTS

I love writing acknowledgments. It brings to mind many of the wonderful people in my life. When it comes to *The Feel the Fear Guide to Lasting Love,* the following were there for me, each in their own way …

Judith Kendra, the Publishing Director of Rider, Random House UK, who was the impetus behind my writing this book. Over the years, she has supported my work in every way, and I am very, very appreciative. Thank you, Judith.

Elizabeth Zack, owner of Bookcrafters, LLC, who did the final edit for the U.S. edition of this book. Her expertise and friendship have been in invaluable.

Tom and SueEllen Strapp of Powersource, my wonderful web-masters. They created **www.susanjeffers.com**, a very happy and successful website, indeed.

Dotti Albertine, who worked so patiently to create the cover and text design for this edition.

Kat Ward, at Spence Studios, for the beautiful photo that appears on the cover. The photos were all so good, it was difficult making a choice.

The men's groups and women's groups who shared so much of themselves. Their generosity and openness was a true measure of their heart.

The men and women from around the world who flood me with letters of thanks and gratitude. I'm sure that when they write me such beautiful letters, or write appreciative reviews on the internet bookstores, or e-mail their thanks, they don't realize what a gift it is that they give to me.

My amazing friends who, each in their own way, have contributed to my thoughts of love as I wrote this book: Caren Lobo, Dick Lobo, Sir Ken and Lady Terry Robinson, Diana Von Welanetz Wentworth, Ted Wentworth, Donna Gradstein, Henry Gradstein, Paul Huson, Bill Bast, Jerry Beckerman, Libby Gill, Mariana Danilovic, Christine Adzich, Stuart McFaul, Melissa Oberon, John Levoff, Larry Gershman, Trevor Chenery, Sue Chenery, Rosie Bunting, Michael Leggo, Joy Starr, Martha Lawrence and Mandi Robbins.

My wonderful family: my son, Gerry Gershman, my daughter, Leslie Wandmacher, my son-in-law, Michael Wandmacher, my step-daughter and son-in-law, Anthony and Alice Shelmerdine, my step-son and daughter-in-law, Guy Shelmerdine and Ashley Jacobs, my adored sister, Marcia Jeffers and brother-in-law, Bruce Rabiner. My appreciation of them all grows and grows. I am very blessed, indeed.

And most importantly, my husband, Mark Shelmerdine, who is the greatest lover in every way. How fantastic to have him in my life!

INTRODUCTION
THE JOURNEY BEGINS

All truths are easy to understand once they
are discovered; the point is to discover them.
—GALILEO GALILEI

M uch of my life's work has been about teaching people how to push through fear in order to move forward in life. It now feels wonderful to be able to show you how we can all push through fear in order to find a beautiful love … and to make it last. This book is for you whether …

- You are not in a relationship and are wondering what you are doing wrong.

- You are in a lacklustre relationship and are looking for ways to create more closeness and caring.

- You are thinking of ending your relationship and are wondering if there is a way to save it.

- You are in a happy relationship and are looking for ways to make it even better.

- You are counselling couples and are looking for new insights.

Whatever your situation, my greatest desire in writing *The Feel the Fear Guide to Lasting Love* is to offer you my thoughts on the meaning of love in its highest sense and to show you how to incorporate the essence of this kind of love into your daily interactions with your present or future mate.

Although most of us desire a healthy relationship, it is surprising how many of us don't really understand the nature of real love. We say we love people in our lives, yet often we don't act very lovingly. It would be comical, if it weren't so sad, how many people hurt others ... and are deeply hurt by others ... in the name of love. This lack of understanding about the meaning of love is reflected in the high rate of divorce and the large number of people who are asking with a deep yearning in their hearts, *"Why is love so hard?"*

Over the years I have come to be known as an expert on love, but it is important for you to know that it took me a while to gain the understanding I now have. While I have a number of university degrees, most of my meaningful knowledge about "real" love came from personal experience. You see my first marriage of sixteen years ended in divorce. And then there were the twelve years of dating before I married again.

Looking back, what a great training ground all those years turned out to be, especially the twelve years in-between my marriages! During that time, I had relationships of varying lengths with numerous men, much to the chagrin of my mother. Of course, my mother never did understand that it was through all these relationships that, s-l-o-w-l-y but surely, I learned the secrets of loving and being loved. Little by little, I whittled away what didn't look like love and ultimately the true picture of love emerged. It was a beautiful sight to behold.

As a result of those important years of learning, my second marriage of nineteen years (as I write this) is wonderful. My daughter, Leslie, who was born during my first marriage, came to my present husband Mark and me on her wedding day and said,

"Thank you for showing me what love looks like." I cannot imagine a greater tribute to our marriage than that.

You may be thinking that the success of my second marriage simply has to do with the differences between the two men I married. While it is true that my first and second husbands are very different, their differences do not necessarily explain the demise of my first marriage and the success of my second. What *does* explain it?

> It is ME that is totally different in my second marriage from the person that I was in my first marriage. *And it is in this difference that I was able to find the secrets of a healthy relationship.*

Yes, it was me that had to learn how to love before I could create a healthy relationship. I was a slow learner, but with the benefit of my experience, I trust you will learn much faster than I did! And learning how to love is what this book is all about.

The process looks like this: First, you have to discover the bad habits that destroy love. Then you have to break these destructive habits and replace them with the good habits that keep love alive and thriving. Little by little, the good replaces the bad and an entirely different (and beautiful!) picture of love emerges. As you read ...

> *You will learn* that one of the primary causes of any problem in a relationship, *or the lack of a relationship,* is fear. As you push through the fear, it becomes much easier to find your way to love.

> *You will learn that* sometimes, because of your habitual ways of acting in your relationship, you cannot see the obvious: you cannot see how your own thoughts and behavior contribute to any unhappiness you are experiencing.

You will learn that it's okay to have problems in a relationship; everyone does. "Life happens" and your relationship offers you much opportunity to learn how to "dance on a shifting carpet."

You will learn that no matter what is happening in your relationship, you can learn from it all; therefore, it's all "good"—even the problems. Your relationship, or lack of one, is truly the best workshop going!

You will learn that if your partner does not want to work on the relationship, *you can work on it alone ... very productively and very happily.* In the end, you are doing the work for yourself anyway, as a pathway to becoming a more loving person.

You will learn how to make your relationship extra-special by including those elements that keep love alive and thriving. The simplest acts of caring can make all the difference in the world.

You will learn when it's time to leave a relationship and when it's worth taking another look.

You will learn that you are more powerful and loving than you ever could have imagined. And once you get in touch with all the power and love you hold inside, your relationship will reap the benefits. And if you are not in a relationship, getting in touch with your inner power and love will help you draw a beautiful person into your life.

What I present within these pages is an ideal way of being in love. Because we are all human, we won't always get it right. Certainly I have my lapses! But as we begin including in our lives more and more components of a beautiful love, we begin to understand the joy, satisfaction, peace and caring that real love can bring.

As you master the techniques in this book, you will notice an additional benefit. Not only will your relationship with your mate improve, *all* of your relationships will improve. When you learn how to open your heart to love, it is felt by everyone around you. That's just the way it is. Also, as you move forward, *the speed of your learning will increase.* That's very good news! Love lessons seem to build upon themselves in an exponential manner. You will be able to embrace the meaning and actions of love faster and faster.

Here are a few suggestions for reaping the benefits of this book:

- I have included many exercises called "Love Lessons" that can help your relationship thrive. I suggest you read through the book in its entirety and note those exercises that seem to draw you to them. They indicate where you should begin. Some of the exercises will work very effectively for you, some will not; we are all different human beings with different needs and preferences.

- Don't feel overwhelmed by the exercises. Remember that this is a step-by-step journey. You don't have to do it all at once. In fact, it is impossible to do it all at once! But, as you have just learned, the learning does get faster and faster as you proceed.

- You will notice that I use the terms "mate," "lover" and "partner" interchangeably to refer to the person you love, whether you are married or not, whether you are in a male/female or same-sex relationship or whether you are in a new or long-term relationship. All the principles apply no matter what form your relationship takes. It's all about love.

• Since both men and women will be reading this book, you will see "he/she" as it relates to your mate. Obviously, if your mate is male, read it as "he" and if your mate is female, read it as "she."

• Don't be put off by my use of the word "power" throughout the book. By power, I don't mean control over others; I mean control over our own actions and reactions, which is a very good thing. Without that power, we are run by fear and a sense of neediness. Not good for a relationship! You can see why "power" and "love" definitely go together. Without a sense of power, it is very difficult to love and be loved.

• You will hear the stories of a number of people, including myself, and their relationship with love. Remember that the stories are here just to illustrate the principles. *It is these principles that you need to take into your being and apply in your everyday life.*

• You will find references to some of my other books where relevant. Yes, I would love you to read my other books. More importantly, I want you to know where you can go to expand your knowledge about the particular point that is referenced.

• You may not agree with everything you read. Not to worry. As I always suggest, take what works for you and let the rest go.

I've structured the book as follows:

Part I: The Basics gives you a picture of what real love looks like. In addition I provide a simple and very effective tool for helping you to move in the right direction. Very importantly, this part of the book also explains how fear often stops us from loving and being loved and how we can push through the fear.

Part II: The Essence gives you the many parts of the "Grand Design" of a beautiful love. You will see that when all of these parts are put together, the simplicity and beauty of love stands before your eyes ... and within your heart.

Part III: Freedom to be ... You and Me provides you with many valuable insights as to how the men's and women's movements affect our relationships today. Understanding and adapting to these life-changing aspects of recent history will save you a lot of unhappiness indeed.

Conclusion: Guess What I Finally Found! gives you a healthy new spin on a very old and outdated yearning that lies deep within our hearts.

Addendum: Take Another Look helps you determine if it's definitely time to leave a relationship or if it's worth taking one more look.

I suggest that you consider your first reading of this book as the beginning of a wonderful journey. Even if you have a great relationship, there is always more to learn. There is so much information contained within the book for you to embrace. As a result, you will want to read it over and over again. And when you've milked as much as you can out of it, refer back to it often. Many of you have told me that you keep *Feel the Fear and Do It Anyway* by your bedside so you can refer to it frequently. I hope you now will be keeping *two* books by your bedside to refer to frequently!

Remember that no matter what the state of your relationship at the present time, it offers you an incredible opportunity for learning and growing. It is definitely worth all the effort you put into it. Why?

A loving relationship feels sublime and brings you great joy; it makes life sweeter and easier. You delight in your ability to give to your mate; you feel abundant as you take in the love that he/she gives to you. Just sharing the journey with someone you love … it doesn't get any better than that.

Yes … it's definitely worth all the effort you put into it.

PART I

THE BASICS

I am creating a beautiful love I am creating a beautiful love I am creating a beautiful love I am creating a beautiful love I am creating a beautiful love I am creating a beautiful love I am creating a beautiful love I am creating a beautiful love I am creating a beautiful love **I am creating a beautiful love** I am creating a beautiful love I am creating a beautiful love I am creating a beautiful love I am creating a beautiful love I am creating a beautiful love I am creating a beautiful love I am creating a beautiful love I am creating a beautiful love I am creating a beautiful love I am creating a beautiful love I am creating a beautiful love I am creating a beautiful love I am creating a beautiful love **I am creating a beautiful love** I am creating a beautiful love I am creating a beautiful love I am creating a beautiful love I am creating a beautiful love I am creating a beautiful love I am creating a beautiful love I am creating a beautiful love I am creating a beautiful love **I am creating a beautiful love** I am creating a beautiful love I am creating a beautiful love I am creating a beautiful love I am creating a beautiful love I am creating a beautiful love I am creating a beautiful love I am creating a beautiful love **I am creating a beautiful love** I am creating a beautiful love I am creating a beautiful love I am creating a beautiful love I am creating a beautiful love I am creating a beautiful love I am creating a beautiful love **I am creating a beautiful love** I am creating a beautiful love I am creating a beautiful love I am

Chapter 1

WHAT DOES *REAL* LOVE *REALLY* LOOK LIKE?

Imagine how much easier it would be for us to learn how to love if we began with a shared definition.

—BELL HOOKS[1]

L ove, mysterious love! You must admit I'm very brave attempting to explain something that people have been trying to explain for thousands of years ... but I decided to feel the fear and explain it anyway! You would have thought that after all this time we would have figured it out. But about real love, most of us are in the dark. And even if we are in a great relationship, there always seems to be so much more to learn.

One of the reasons real love seems so hard to understand is this:

> We in Western society have constantly been fed misleading pictures of what real love actually looks like.

Let me remind you of what is considered the greatest love story ever told, *Romeo and Juliet*, the tale of two dysfunctional fourteen-year-olds who would rather kill themselves than obey their parents! How this story became the model of "the greatest love story" I will never know.

And then there are the fairy tales that omit so many essential truths about love. If you have children, I'll wager you felt it your duty to read them the classics—*Cinderella, Beauty and the Beast, Snow White* and the like—just as your parents once read them to you. Hmm. Think about it: Fairy tales always focus on some version of our hero and heroine falling madly in love, walking off into the distance and supposedly living happily after. But do they live happily after? Maybe they do; maybe they don't.

This doesn't stop young people today from hoping. For example, the news recently featured a lovely charity in the U.S. called Becca's Closet.[2] Among other services, it provides gowns for young women who can't afford them so that they can attend their graduation ball with their classmates. As one young woman was modeling her beautiful new gown, she exclaimed, "I feel like Cinderella in this dress." I thought to myself, "Some things never change!"

One of my favorite Broadway musicals is *Into the Woods*.[3] One of the major characters in this delightful play is Cinderella and, true to the story, she gets to marry her prince. But the play dares to take us into the future where we learn that, alas, the Prince has a roving eye and the relationship ends. What a blow! What happened to living happily ever after? Certainly whatever magic it was that brought them together soon disappeared. But all is not lost, as Cinderella learns a very good lesson: She will have to look at love in a much more eyes-wide-open manner the next time around. Could this be our new version of a happy ending?

And then there are the multitude of stories we hear about "love at first sight." Let's look at it logically: *How can you love someone when you don't even know them?* That "stranger across a crowded room" could be someone you should *definitely* avoid.

And we can't forget the misleading concept of "falling in love?" Don't we realize that when we fall, we can get hurt? As well-known relationship expert and television personality, Dr. Phil McGraw humorously points out:

> We describe the start of new romance as "falling" in love. *"Fall: verb, to go from high to lower ground, usually in an out-of-control fashion."* Hmm, it's also a word we use to describe times when we've been suckered, as in, "I was so stupid to fall for that!"[4]

Yes, it seems we are stupid to fall for that—which can be explained by the mysterious fact that love at first sight can feel so good ... *while it lasts.* I remember it well: I was walking down the street one day in New York City. The freshness of spring was in the air and all was well. It was during the period between my marriages and I was feeling particularly free and happy. At some point, I noticed an extremely handsome man walking in my direction. He was hard to miss. Our eyes connected and ... WOW! All my passionate urges came to the fore. We maintained eye contact until we passed each other by. I smiled, took a deep breath and said to myself, "WHAT was that?" I had walked only a few steps further when I felt someone tap me on the shoulder. I turned around. And there we were ... face to face. At that very moment, it happened: We "fell in love." And thus began one of the most passionate and crazy six months of my life.

But, alas, as time went by, whatever created this passionate and crazy attraction wore off. The "spell" was broken. And as always happens when the spell is broken, we woke up to reality. Our humanness was revealed to each other, and since neither of us understood the process of creating real love, we were soon embroiled in constant bouts of judgment, anger, annoyance and other such love-destroying emotions. The situation worsened until I reached the point where I no longer wanted him in my life. I remember the relief I felt when I asked him to leave my apartment and never contact me again. As the door shut behind him, I once again smiled, took a deep breath and said to myself, "WHAT was that?" A very good question, indeed.

Over the years, I have come to call this kind of love "enchanted love." Indeed, enchantment can be defined as a spell that comes over us. And that's exactly what seems to happen when we experience love at first sight. It is mystical, exciting, passionate and delicious ... BUT ... it is not real love. I don't have a clue as to why enchanted love occurs. It is amazingly irrational. What is most confusing is the fact that so many couples who are caught in its spell are definitely *not* good candidates for a long-term relationship.

Interestingly, a number of sources report that the spell that seems to come over us when we are in the throes of enchanted love is actually caused by a peptide called PEA (phenoethalymine) that is created within the body. (How unromantic is that!) Some attribute it to a neurotransmitter called dopamine which is also created within the body. Both of these "love potions" somehow create amazing feelings of passion, energy, joy and all good things. Hmm. Maybe the love potion theory is true; maybe it isn't. Even if it is true, I haven't seen any explanation as to why these potions suddenly pop up in your body when you gaze into the eyes of a complete stranger. More research is definitely necessary!

It is also reported that these love potions *always* wear off, usually in six months to two years. This is a good thing! Enchanted love is a *destructive* kind of love in that it is all-consuming and messes up other areas of our lives. We ignore our friends, our jobs, our plans, our beliefs and other of those things that contribute to the richness of our lives. (Does this sound familiar?) As playwright George Bernard Shaw once said of such a love:

> "I can't imagine anyone wanting such a debilitating emotion to last forever."

I agree. I often have joked that when you see that proverbial stranger across a crowded room you should turn around and run the other way. In reality, it is certainly possible to turn enchanted love into real love. I've seen it happen many times. It requires that we first allow the spell of enchanted love to wear off. As reality sets in, we can see more clearly and then decide if we want to move forward with the relationship … or end it. If we choose to go forward, it is then that the journey to real love truly can begin. In such a way, enchanted love can ultimately become real love, but for obvious reasons, it is not wise to get married when under the spell of enchanted love: It may all fall apart when the enchantment wears off!

It is also important to point out that real love doesn't require an initial period of enchantment. In fact:

Some of the best examples of real love are between two people who weren't particularly attracted to each other when they originally met.

I've heard many happy couples report that in the beginning their mates were "not their type." Certainly when I met Mark, my second husband, he definitely was not my type. He jokes that when we first started dating, I wouldn't even invite him in for a coffee and cuddle. But, little by little, I saw what a wonderful man he was. The happy ending was that he eventually got his coffee and his cuddle, and our journey to real love began.

And what is real love all about? One of my favorite pictures of real love comes from psychologist Robert Johnson. In his book, WE, he talks about "stirring-the-oatmeal love." He says:

"To 'stir the oatmeal' means to find the relatedness, the value, even the beauty, in simple and ordinary things, not to eternally demand a cosmic drama, an entertainment, or an extraordinary intensity in everything. Like the rice hulling of the Zen monks, the spinning wheel of Ghandi, the tent making of Saint Paul, it represents the discovery of the sacred in the midst of the humble and ordinary."[5]

"The sacred in the midst of the humble and ordinary." Beautiful! When I read this, I was overcome with a deep sense of "knowingness." After many years of marriage, Mark and I experience so many "stirring the oatmeal" moments together. Something as simple as sitting down to dinner at the end of the day with the candles lit and a toast to each other that says "I love you and I thank you" gives us a true piece of heaven on earth. How did Mark and I come to the place where just eating dinner, watching television, taking a walk, enjoying our neighborhood and doing all the ordinary things that people do bring us so much joy? Certainly we didn't reach this point overnight. It took years of learning.

I have at times heard the erroneous concept that you shouldn't have to work on love. "If you have to work on it, it isn't real love." I disagree. The reality is that we are all human beings who are very often run by the weakest and most insecure part of who we are—our Lower Self. Our goal in a relationship is to learn how to rise to the most powerful and loving part of who we are—our Higher Self. This takes time; it takes focus; it takes an open mind; and, most importantly, it takes an understanding of what loving another person really means. If this understanding isn't there, very often the relationship breaks down.

So many relationships start out with a commitment to love each other forever. But when the so-called honeymoon stage wears off and life interferes, the relationship often ends. Bob's story is typical. He got married at a very early age. Just six weeks after his wedding, he and his wife were out to dinner with some friends. Someone joked that he should enjoy it while it lasts, as so many people end up divorced. He remembers responding to his friend, "That will never happen to us." And he truly believed the marriage would never end. But it did end. Five years later. What happened? He and his wife grew apart as petty differences interfered with their togetherness and they never learned how to put themselves back together again. What Bob and his wife didn't know was this:

Commitment doesn't mean you stop learning how to love. It is quite the opposite: *Commitment is where the really important learning needs to begin.*

Read this again … and again!

As I see it, a relationship has two very important purposes—a Practical Purpose and a Higher Purpose.

The Practical Purpose of a relationship is simply to have someone with whom to share our lives. Traveling the road together can be a truly joyous experience. It feels wonderful to have a loving partner by your side in good times and in bad. But sometimes problems with money, sex, children, work and the like can make the journey together very difficult. *It is for this reason that we need to have a Higher Purpose.*

The Higher Purpose of a relationship is our commitment to learn how to become a more loving person—despite what problems come up. It is our *using* all the problems as a vehicle for seeing what we need to work on within ourselves to keep love in our heart. This Higher Purpose is also about learning to pay attention to all the good in our relationship. Too many of us don't even seem to notice the good.

The Practical Purpose of a relationship is obvious; the Higher Purpose too often is not. And unless we learn, understand and always keep in mind our Higher Purpose, the relationship may suffer. Make no mistake about it. Too often, without remembering our Higher Purpose, we begin longing for the initial bloom of love and the downward spiral begins. We blame our mate instead of realizing that this is a great time for learning and growing. The criticism, sarcasm, put-downs and other love-destroying behavior escalate. We become annoyed, disillusioned and disappointed. Anger and resentment build. We find ourselves stuck in what I

17

call "selfish love" and we soon begin to wonder why we are in the relationship at all. And for many of us, it is safe to predict that the end is near.

If, however, we focus on the Higher Purpose of our relationship, *that of becoming a more loving person,* the outcome can be very different. We learn, we grow, we are filled with creativity, we take responsibility, we feel strong and our love for our mate grows and grows. There is no question that it is through our Higher Purpose that we ultimately experience the exquisite beauty of real love. To keep you focused on your Higher Purpose, I have included many Love Lessons at the end of each chapter. If you begin practicing these Love Lessons, in a very short time you will begin to notice a dramatic difference in the quality of your relationship.

Selfish love is a product of our Lower Self, which is ego-based and—subtly or not so subtly—creates a need to control and a need to get instead of give. Real love is a product of our Higher Self, which is heart-based and creates a beautiful sense of partnership, giving and growing up in love, all of which will be explained in the course of this book.

Real love is an amazing gift we give to ourselves and to our mate. And because we are all human, we won't always get it right. As situations change in our lives, we have to keep fine-tuning. But as we focus on our Higher Purpose, that of becoming a more loving person, we begin to understand the joy, satisfaction, peace and caring that real love can bring.

It is important to know and keep in mind the main ingredients of real love. Without including them as an integral part of your relationship, it is doubtful that real love can become a reality. Here is a list of what I consider the most important of these ingredients:

VALIDATION
Real love can't exist in an environment
of negative judgment and putdowns.

RESPONSIBILITY
Real love can't exist when
we blame our mate for our unhappiness.

APPRECIATION
Real love can't exist in the absence of "thank you's."

A RESPECT BASED ON THE
HUMANNESS OF OUR PARTNERS
Real love can't exist with fairy-tale expectations.

COMMITMENT
Real love can't exist when one foot is out the door.

INTEGRITY
Real love can't exist when we don't honor
the welfare—physically and emotionally—of our partner.

COMFORT
Real love can't exist when tension
permeates the relationship.

AN OPEN HEART
Real love can't exist when we shut the door to
the beauty that lies within our being … and theirs.

ALONE-TIME TOGETHER
Real love requires sacred time for two lovers
to focus on and appreciate the beauty of each other.

COMMUNICATION
Real love requires that we connect from
a place of sharing, caring and learning.

KINDNESS
Real love can't exist when we are oblivious
to the pain we are causing our mate.

CELEBRATION
Real love can't exist when we take
the blessings of our union for granted.

I might add that while these components may seem an obvious requirement for a healthy and fulfilling love, *it is amazing how many of us don't see or act on what is obvious*. Many of these components are absent from the lives of many couples who claim to love one another. Little do they know that, without these ingredients being integrated into their relationship, their love can't last.

My intention in the pages that follow is to open your eyes so that you can see why you are missing the "love-boat" if you are not working to include these beautiful components of real love into your relationship. Having missed the love-boat a number of times myself, I know what I am talking about. Thankfully, I finally climbed aboard.

You now have a sense of what real love is all about. And as you read, your understanding will become clearer and clearer. Again, I believe that when many of us enter into a relationship, we don't really know how to love. It is when the original feeling of bliss is over that the learning begins. And as we train ourselves to focus on our Higher Purpose, that of becoming a more loving person, we are able to push through our negative habits and emerge as strong and caring human beings. In this way, step by step, day by day, our love can grow … and grow … and grow.

LOVE LESSON

1) *Imprint your Higher Purpose on your mind.* Constantly remind yourself that:

The most important purpose of this relationship is for me to learn how to become a more loving person.

Repeat this over and over again so that when you find yourself embroiled in a problem in the relationship, it will lead you to loving solutions instead of feelings of hostility. As you continue to embody your Higher Purpose in all your interactions, the likelihood is greatly increased that your relationship will more than grow ... it will flourish!

feel the fear and do it any way feel the fear and do it anyway feel the fear and do it anyway feel the fear and do it anyway feel the fear and do it anyway feel the fear and do it anyway feel the fear and do it anyway feel the fear and do it anyway feel the fear and do it anyway feel the fear and do it anyway feel the fear and do it anyway feel the fear and do it anyway feel the fear and do it anyway feel the fear and do it anyway feel the fear and do it any way **feel the fear and do it any way** feel the fear and do it anyway feel the fear and do it anyway feel the fear and do it anyway feel the fear and do it any-way feel the fear and do it anyway feel the fear and do it anyway feel the fear and do it anyway feel the fear and do it anyway feel the fear and do it anyway feel the fear and do it anyway feel the fear and do it anyway feel the fear and do it anyway feel the fear and do it any way feel the fear and do it any way **feel the fear and do it anyway** feel the fear and do it anyway feel the fear and do it anyway feel the fear and do it anyway feel the fear and do it anyway feel the fear and do it anyway feel the fear and do it anyway feel the fear and do it anyway feel the fear and do it anyway feel the fear and do it anyway feel the fear and do it anyway feel the fear and do it anyway feel the fear and do it anyway **feel the fear and do it any way** feel the fear and do it anyway feel the fear and do it anyway feel the fear and do it anyway feel the fear and do it anyway feel the fear and do it anyway feel the fear and do it anyway feel the fear and do it anyway feel the fear and do it anyway feel the fear and do it any way feel the fear and do it anyway **feel the fear and do it any way** feel the fear and do it anyway feel the fear and do it anyway

Chapter 2

HOW FEAR SUBTLY DESTROYS LOVE

You overcome weakness by leaving it behind you.
This means that you become aware of the inner ten-
dencies that bring you down, that do not support a
belief in self, that do not endorse a love of self, and
you say, 'I don't want to be that any more.' You then
move yourself out of the slovenly ways of the collec-
tive unconscious, into a discipline of power.
                                    —STUART WILDE[1]

There is no question that to love freely and joyfully, we need to push through our fear of loving. You may be thinking, "Susan, what does fear have to do with love?" It is my belief that if you are having trouble in your relationship, fear is definitely involved. Think of it this way:

Fear causes us to protect ourselves.
Love requires us to become "safely vulnerable," in the knowledge that we can handle whatever happens.

23

Fear is rigidly holding on in desperation.
Love is relaxing and letting love flow.

Fear causes us to close our hearts.
Love is about opening our hearts.

Fear causes us always to put ourselves first.
Love is knowing when and how to put our loved one first.

Fear creates judgment.
Love creates compassion.

Fear creates blame.
Love requires that we take charge of our thoughts and actions and change what doesn't work for us.

Fear creates anger, discord and coldness between the sexes.
Love creates a feeling of harmony, warmth and love.

Let me add this all up:

Fear causes us to protect ourselves, to rigidly hold on, to close our hearts, to put our needs first often at the expense of our mates, to judge them and blame them for our unhappiness, and to spread our free-floating anger to all members of the opposite sex ... particularly our mates. Not a pretty picture!

Love, on the other hand, comes from a feeling of inner strength that allows us to relax and to let love flow, to open our hearts, to reap the rewards of putting our loved ones first, to understand and have compassion for the humanness of our mates, to take responsibility for our reactions to all things, and to create a feeling of harmony and love with all members of the opposite sex ... particularly our mates. A beautiful picture indeed!

Are you convinced? Hopefully, you can see that as we learn to push through our fears, whatever they may be, the miracle of love stands brilliantly before us.

The reason why we seldom realize that fear is getting in the way of love is that fear has an amazing ability to hide itself behind other emotions, such as anger, blame, judgment and the like. Let me give you an example of how this works: Tom was a man in his forties who found himself constantly annoyed and closed off from his wife. The situation was so bad that his wife finally persuaded him to come for marriage counseling. There he complained that she was too controlling ... she wanted them to be together too much of the time ... he was afraid of being engulfed ... he needed his space ... and on and on and on.

With the help of the marriage counselor he was able to get to the bottom of his upset. Beneath it all *he was frightened that if he totally opened his heart to his wife, she might leave him and he would be devastated.* The result of his fear of abandonment was that he did everything to keep his distance. Wow! This was a big discovery that totally surprised him.

When he finally realized what was behind his inability to connect with his wife, Tom knew what his next step had to be ... and that was to build his sense of confidence in himself. In this way he could become "safely vulnerable," knowing he would get to the other side of any pain he would feel, if, for some reason the relationship ended. I might add that the marriage counselor was very wise in digging deeper and deeper to get to the heart of Tom's fear.

You can see how destructive fear is when it is hidden from our consciousness, but how instructive it is when it is out in the open right before our eyes. Our reasons for fear are many ... but let me now wrap up all these fears into ONE BIG FEAR that explains it all. If you have read *Feel the Fear and Do It Anyway,* you're already way ahead of me. You'll recall the following:

At the bottom of every one of your fears is simply the fear that you can't handle whatever life may bring you ... If you knew you could handle anything that came your way, what would you possibly have to fear? The answer is: NOTHING![2]

Read this again and again and again. It is this understanding that sets the course for what you need to do to diminish your fear when it comes to love: Move yourself from the weakest part of who you are, your Lower Self, to the strongest part of who you are, your Higher Self. It then looks like this:

FEAR-BASED QUESTION	HIGHER SELF ANSWER
What if he/she leaves me?	Whatever happens, I'll handle it!
What if he/she has an affair?	Whatever happens, I'll handle it!
What if I lose my identity?	Whatever happens, I'll handle it!
What if I lose my freedom?	Whatever happens, I'll handle it!
What if I ask for what I need and I don't get it?	Whatever happens, I'll handle it!

You can see how important it is to collect—and then use—the tools that build that vital confidence in yourself so that when the "what-if's" come up, you can simply tell yourself, "Whatever happens, I'll handle it!"

I have provided Higher Self tools for handling fear in almost all of my books, particularly in *Feel the Fear and Do It Anyway, Feel the Fear ... And Beyond,* and *Embracing Uncertainty.* Exercises for pushing through fear abound in these books. I even co-wrote *"I Can Handle It!"* to help young children push through their fears.[3] (I don't know how many people have said to me, "I wish I had learned all of this stuff earlier.") And, of course, I will be providing many Higher Self tools (Love Lessons) throughout this book as well.

So you have no excuse not to handle your fear. The tools are certainly available. Your task now is first to *recognize* that fear is in some way behind any problems you may be having when it comes to your relationship. It is then time to use your favorite tools to move you to a place of power and love—your Higher Self—where you truly know you can handle it all.

Making these tools an integral part of who you are in your relationship is very important, and repetition is the key. Practice. Practice. Practice. While practice doesn't make perfect, it definitely goes a heck of a long way! My experience of love has taught me that the more I am able to think in a Higher Self way, the more joyous is my relationship.

So begin filling your toolbox with tools that take you to all the power and love you hold inside. Yes, "life happens" and new fears come up, but when we have our tools at hand, we always know there is peace on the other side of the pain. When you realize that you can handle whatever happens in your relationship, you will understand what being "safely vulnerable" is all about. It's a magnificent feeling, as it frees us to relax into the comfort and beauty of a loving relationship—which, I might add, is a feeling like no other.

Psychotherapist David Richo wrote the following moving words specifically for men:

> "We men have been taught to concentrate on being brave and strong. But the fear that gets in the way of our being strong doesn't matter as much as the fear that gets in the way of loving, because love is the most precious strength a man can have. May we care about becoming loving more than anything else in life."[4]

I suggest that women adapt and embrace the message of this quote for themselves as well. We must all—men and women alike—push through the fear that gets in the way of love. We must all "care about becoming loving more than anything else in life." This is our Higher Purpose in action. This is our guarantee for a beautiful life ... and a beautiful love.

LOVE LESSONS

1) *Recognize the best of who you are.* As many of you already know, I love affirmations. *Affirmations* are simply strong positive statements that quiet the negativity of the Lower Self and introduce you to the power of the Higher Self. When we repeat affirmations often enough, we actually begin to believe them. I have written extensively about affirmations. In fact, I've created a number of affirmation books and tapes.[5] The following affirmation, which relates to pushing through our fear of loving and being loved, is a perfect one to get you started:

**I am powerful and loving
and I have nothing to fear.**

Repeat it at least ten times three times a day … morning, noon and night … especially before you go to sleep. Eventually, these empowering words begin to roam through your head when negativity threatens to invade your peace of mind. Don't be concerned if you don't believe that you are powerful and loving and have nothing to fear. An affirmation is a form of "act-as-if." Trust me when I tell you that if you act-as-if long enough, you begin to realize that it is absolutely so!

2) *Learn the power of saying "YES!" to the Universe.* Saying YES! is another of my favorite tools that works beautifully when it comes to love. To me, it simply and importantly means that:

**Whatever happens in my relationship,
I will learn and grow from it all.**

That is YES! in its highest sense. In practice, this means that if you are having a problem, your task is to commit to finding ways to make it a plus in your life instead of a negative. It is from

28

problems that we can learn so much and become more loving as a result. That's beautiful! There is enormous power in saying YES!

I suggest you write down the things you most fear in terms of your relationship—or lack of one. After each of these fears, add this powerful statement:

I can say YES! to this. Whatever happens, I will use it to enrich my life in some way. I will learn from it; I will grow from it. Somehow, I will find a way to use it to become a more loving and powerful person.

Saying YES! is building trust in your ability to handle all that life hands you. And as your trust in yourself grows, your relationship can become more loving than you ever thought it could be.

I radiate love I radiate love I radiate love I radiate love
I radiate love **I radiate love** I radiate love I radiate love
I radiate love I radiate love I radiate love I radiate love
I radiate love I radiate love I radiate love I radiate love
I radiate love I radiate love I radiate love I radiate love
I radiate love I radiate love I radiate love I radiate love
I radiate love I radiate love **I radiate love** I radiate love
I radiate love I radiate love I radiate love I radiate love
I radiate love I radiate love I radiate love I radiate love
I radiate love I radiate love I radiate love I radiate love
I radiate love I radiate love I radiate love I radiate love
I radiate love I radiate love I radiate love I radiate love
I radiate love I radiate love I radiate love I radiate love
I radiate love I radiate love I radiate love I radiate love
I radiate love I radiate love I radiate love I radiate love
I radiate love I radiate love I radiate love I radiate love
I radiate love I radiate love I radiate love I radiate love
I radiate love I radiate love I radiate love **I radiate love**
I radiate love I radiate love I radiate love I radiate love
I radiate love I radiate love I radiate love I radiate love
I radiate love **I radiate love** I radiate love I radiate love
I radiate love I radiate love I radiate love I radiate love
I radiate love I radiate love I radiate love I radiate love
I radiate love I radiate love I radiate love I radiate love
I radiate love I radiate love I radiate love I radiate love
I radiate love I radiate love I radiate love I radiate love
I radiate love I radiate love I radiate love I radiate love
I radiate love I radiate love **I radiate love** I radiate love
I radiate love I radiate love I radiate love I radiate love
I radiate love I radiate love I radiate love I radiate love
I radiate love I radiate love I radiate love I radiate love
I radiate love I radiate love I radiate love I radiate love
I radiate love I radiate love I radiate love I radiate love
I radiate love I radiate love I radiate love I radiate love
I radiate love I radiate love I radiate love I radiate love

Chapter 3

IT ONLY TAKES ONE

We must become the change we want to see.
—MAHATMA GHANDI

Now that you are coming to the realization that you are power-ful and loving and have nothing to fear, I invite you to use your power and love in a creative and exciting way … and that is to work toward improving your relationship (or finding one) *all by yourself.*

I can hear some objections out there. Some of you are angry because your mate won't work on your relationship with you. I have heard it said many times, "I'm tired of working on the rela-tionship all by myself!" May I suggest that if this applies to you, by definition, *the way you are working on the relationship all by yourself, is definitely not working!* You need a new approach. You need to open your heart and your mind and learn a fresh new way of relating to your mate. It may save your relationship, and it will certainly make you a happier person.

Yes, it is wonderful when both partners in a relationship work together on various issues that are getting in the way of love. Many of our partners are willing, if not eager, to do that with us. But it is no less wonderful to take on the challenge of seeing what you can do on your own. Even though everything in this book can be shared, I wrote it as a *self-help* guide. You *can* do it alone. There is great power in that knowledge.

Whether your relationship is in good shape and simply needs some fine-tuning, or whether your relationship is in serious trouble, you will be amazed at how much relationship-healing you can do all by yourself. And if you are not in a relationship, the ideas in this book will certainly help you to approach members of the opposite sex in a new and welcoming manner. So let's begin!

The first order of the day is for you to keep your Higher Purpose in mind at all times. I'll repeat it here just in case you have forgotten it already. (How quickly we forget!)

The most important purpose of my relationship is to learn how to become a more loving person.

This sounds like an ideal goal, yet I can guarantee that resistance from your Lower Self, the weakest part of who you are, will often surface as you proceed, especially in the beginning. But don't worry. As you keep at it, there will come a time when loving will seem like the more natural way to go.

Keeping your Higher Purpose in mind, let me begin by telling you something that may or may not surprise you, and that is:

FEELINGS ARE CONTAGIOUS.

What do I mean by that? I know it is hard to imagine, but we don't end where our skin ends. We have a certain radiance, energy or aura that "touches" the people around us. "Susan, don't give me any of this woo-woo stuff," I hear you say. But it's not woo-woo stuff at all. Think about it this way:

We have all been with people whom it feels really good to be around. These people radiate a positive aura. They are light-hearted, caring, interested in other people and very huggable.

We've also all been with people whom it feels really bad to be around. These people radiate a negative aura. They are self-involved complainers and blamers, and you really want to keep your distance from them.

The obvious implication, of course, is that it would be great if we could fine-tune our own thoughts, actions and behavior so that we radiate a welcoming aura (light-hearted, caring, interested and very huggable) to all those around us, especially to our mate. It makes sense, doesn't it?

If you don't think it makes sense, it may help to consider the teachings of psychologist Henry Grayson, amongst others. He tells us that there is scientific evidence, particularly in the fields of quantum mechanics and particle physics, that we are all connected in a most profound way. He also says that there is a "consciousness" or "intelligence" that underlies all that is visible, and that this consciousness gives us human powers beyond our imagination. He concludes that:

> "If we as human beings are all interconnected, then there are enormous implications for understanding how relationships work—both positively and negatively."[1]

He adds that he came to understand how someone else's behavior is often a mirror of our own behavior. So if we are critical, even if only in our thoughts, we will get criticism back. If we have loving thoughts, on the other hand, it brings love toward us. (Read that again.)

Grayson tells of a "far-reaching" experiment he tried with his wife. For one week, without her knowledge, he thought negative thoughts about her during the day. When he came home in the evening, he found that her actions reflected what he was thinking! She was very negative from the minute he walked in the door. For the next week, he thought only loving thoughts about her during the day. When he came home, she was filled with a sense of love for him.[2] Amazing! I don't want to try this experiment with Mark, as I don't want to think negative thoughts about him for a week, nor do I suggest that you do this either, but I'm glad that Grayson tried it for us. We owe him and his wife our thanks!

As a result of his personal experimentation, Grayson concluded that, "I was receiving back what I was thinking inside." This, of course, means that the thoughts in our minds most profoundly affect our relationships. If this is true, it is an awesome realization—that, in terms of our thoughts, we can single-handedly help to create the kinds of feelings we want in our relationship.

Given what you have just learned, it's time to ask yourself an important question:

> "When I am with my mate, do I generally radiate
> a positive energy or a negative energy toward
> him/her?"

Be truthful with yourself. If you have a great relationship, I will wager your answer is that you generally radiate a positive energy. And if you have a lot of problems in your relationship, I will wager your answer is that you generally radiate a negative energy. If the latter describes you, then you know your first challenge: it is to move your thoughts into a more loving place. It stands to reason that:

> *If you think and act lovingly,* your partner will "catch" that
> loving energy. You become a model that evokes love in
> your mate. And the whole nature of the relationship begins
> to move in the direction of love.

If you think and act un-lovingly, your partner will "catch" that un-loving energy. You become a model that evokes conflict in your mate. And the whole nature of the relationship moves itself in the direction of conflict.

You notice that I am not asking you about the energy of your mate. In your journey toward becoming a more loving person, the thoughts and behavior of your mate are not the issue ... *at least not initially.* Your focus needs to be on your own thoughts and behavior. In any case, you have probably learned by now that trying to change another person rarely, if ever, works. But as you begin changing your own thoughts and behavior in the direction of love, it is possible that the whole nature of the relationship will move in the right direction. This is because:

As you become a more loving person, you become *an instrument through which your partner can experience love.* **He or she often becomes more loving as a result.**

Read that again. It is important.

At one point in the writing of this book, I was invited to attend a women's group when visiting a freind in Florida. The topic for the evening was love. Before the discussion began, I witnessed a lovely group of women chatting, laughing and eating the snacks the hostess for the evening had beautifully prepared. When the discussion about love began, very quickly the "aura" of the women changed as they talked about their own relationships—or lack of one.

Predictably the women in the group who were unhappy in their relationships emitted a "miserable" energy—blame, blame, blame. Everyone in the room felt it. One particular woman, Iris, comes to mind. Iris was rigid, negative and filled with disgust. She claimed she was tired of working on the relationship alone. It soon became clear that her idea of working on the relationship alone consisted totally of her efforts to change HIM! It was as if the negativity in the relationship had nothing to do with her. I'm sure her husband "caught" her negative energy as she bludgeoned him with blame. *At no time, even when encouraged by other women in the group, was there any attempt on Iris's part to look at herself to figure out where her deep anger toward him came from.* Not good! Iris certainly was a great example to the other women of how *not* to be in a relationship.

Predictably the women in the group who were in good relationships emitted a very calm, centered, loving and wise energy as they talked about their relationships. You could feel their deep appreciation of their mates. And blame was noticeably absent. One woman, Sally, who had been married for twenty years, had this to say:

> "I know that when I am feeling negatively about something in the relationship, it usually has little to do with him. It has something to do with me. Usually, I just absent myself for a little while until I figure it out. Then once again, all is well."

Sally demonstrates how a relationship can be a fantastic vehicle for self-knowledge. She went on to talk about the many ways her husband enriched her life. Sally definitely had a loving aura around her. I'm sure her husband "caught" her loving aura and responded in kind. As a result, she was able to create a beautiful cycle of love. Interestingly, her husband arrived to collect her at the end of the evening and the energy between them was wonderfully loving, indeed.*

The above demonstrates just one way that we can begin to change our relationship all by ourselves. Again, if your mate wants to work on the relationship with you, that's great. But you

---

*I might add that the single women in the group emitted a "confused" energy. One single woman asked the very significant question, "Can anyone tell me what love feels like?" If you are someone with the same question, hopefully you'll find some answers in the reading of this book.

will be amazed at what you can do on your own. This should be a relief to those of you who have mates who, for their own reasons, are uncomfortable about working on the relationship. However, if you are someone who is annoyed at having to do it alone, it helps to look at it this way:

YOU ARE DOING IT *FOR YOURSELF*!

Think about it. When we ask the question, "Why doesn't he/she change?" we are asking a powerless question. In fact, any pointing of the finger is a powerless act. We must get it into our heads that *we have no power over what other people do.* Real power comes from asking ourselves what changes we *personally* can make to improve the situation. That gives us control. The question we should be asking is:

"What can *I* do to change what isn't
working in this relationship?"

That's powerful, indeed! And, if someone is treating us very badly, the powerless question is: "Why is he/she doing this to me?" The powerful, responsible question is: "How can I build up my confidence enough to leave?" In this way, YOU ARE IN CONTROL.

I'm belaboring this point because I truly believe that our mind plays a very important role in our creating or destroying love. Once you've accepted the fact that your mind controls so much of the quality of your relationship (and your life), the step-by-step process of "changing your mind" makes total sense. And I will provide you with many tools to do this as you move through this book.

If you still believe that it's all his/her fault, then read the above again … and again … and again. Always remember that when you think that it's all the fault of your partner, you give away all your power to make any changes. It's definitely time to take back your power!

As you push through the insecurities that keep your anger and other negative emotions alive, you will find within yourself a more harmonious and loving way of being in your relationship—and in the world. In so doing *you become a person who thinks and acts from your Higher Self (the best of who you are) instead of your Lower Self (the weakest part of who you are).* What could be better than that?

As you can see, we ALL need to be doing it for ourselves. Why be miserable when we can be happy? Hmm. That's a question we constantly need to ask ourselves. Fortunately, the following Love Lessons will point you in the right direction to becoming a happier person with a vibrant aura!

LOVE LESSONS

1) **S*top blaming your mate if he/she does not want to work on the relationship with you.*** Understand that there may be many reasons why he/she is feeling this way, for example, fear of the relationship ending, denial that there's a problem, lack of time and so on. It's good to remember that:

When you stop insisting that your mate work on the relationship with you, *you will immediately feel a sense of freedom to do the work on your own. You are in control!*

Also remind yourself that the insistence that both of you have to work on the relationship is often a cop-out. It may consciously or unconsciously be giving you an excuse for not doing what it takes to change what isn't working—which sometimes takes a lot of courage. It can be much easier to blame our mate and stay miserable than to take responsibility for looking inside and pushing through the fear of changing what needs to be changed within ourselves. Such was the case for Iris, the very unhappy woman I described earlier. Remember, we all have the power to take responsibility for our lives and change what doesn't work.

2) ***Send "I love you" messages.*** To begin changing any negative energy you may be sending to your mate, try the following:

a) First, when you are apart from your mate, close your eyes and picture him or her in front of you. Then silently repeat the words "I love you" over and over again in rapid succession:

**I love you I love you I love you I love you
I love you I love you I love you I love you
I love you I love you I love you I love you**

I warn you that this exercise has been known to bring up rage, tears and all forms of resistance. But keep saying the words *even if you don't mean them.* Your goal is to keep saying them until it feels comfortable. This may take a few days—or more. Be diligent. Don't stop until, in your mind's eye, you are able to easily say "I love you" to your mate. Of course, some of you will do this with no difficulty at all—a good sign that your energy (aura) is moving forward on the road to love.

b) Once you are comfortable saying "I love you" when you are apart from your mate, follow the same process when the two of you are together: Sitting at the dinner table, lying in bed, watching a movie together, or whatever, silently repeat the words "I love you" to your mate over and over again in rapid succession. Again, for some this will be easy, even delicious. For others it will be a process involving pain. But keep at it until it's comfortable.

c) Now it's time for "I love you" to come out in the open. Some of us say, "I love you" to our mates many times a day. But, for a variety of reasons, many of us find it hard to utter these words out loud. If you are serious about keeping love alive, then it is important that you train yourself to say these three very important words, eyeball to eyeball, to your mate. I agree that it would be nice to get an "I love you, too" in response, but for the purposes of this exercise, you are not looking for a response. He/she may or may not respond. Again, you have no control over his/her reactions; you only have control over your actions—and reactions.

Note: If you are disappointed that you don't hear any "I love you" in return, realize it's just something else you need to work on. Ask yourself:

"Why don't I have patience?"
"Why do I have a hard time giving love?"
"Why do I always expect something back in return?"
"Why can't I interpret the loving things
he/she does for me as love?"

You will learn the answers to these questions as you continue reading.

3) *Commit to learning the tools of love.* As you continue to read this book, keep a notebook handy so that you can jot down ideas as to how to put love back into your heart and mind so you can approach your relationship from a position of power and love. How easy it is for us to forget! The words you need to keep repeating to yourself, over and over again, are:

"I am learning exactly what I need to learn."

As you keep repeating these important words, your subconscious mind will be alert and advise you at the proper time, "Here's a good one! Try this one." And your repertoire will grow and grow. Of course, your next step is to USE the tools you are collecting.

4) *Diffuse your negative thoughts.* There are ways to lighten the negativity you are feeling in your mind. In *Embracing Uncertainty*, I provide a Diffuse the Bad News Exercise. I've adapted it here as the "Diffuse the Bad Thoughts Exercise." It works like this. Any time you are feeling something negative, insert something positive. For example:

"It annoys me that she is such a nag. But I can't forget how she shows her love in so many other ways."

41

"It annoys me that the toilet seat is always up. But I can't forget how bad I would feel if the toilet seat was always down ... and he was not a part of my life."*

Right now, think of something that annoys you about your mate and counter this negative feeling with a positive thought. As you do this, you will be radiating this "softening" of your feelings to your mate. This is a very good step toward creating a loving aura.

5) *Notice the behavior of your friends.* If your friends are always complaining about their relationships, it is time to find new friends. You want to be around positive people who appreciate the beauty of their mates and who are working hard to learn as much as they can about becoming more loving people. The complainers in life are not working on becoming more loving people. They are caught in their ever-descending cycle of negativity. In any case, as you learn to enjoy the good feelings that positive thoughts bring you, you will no longer want to be around negative people! Certainly that's the way it was for me.

---

*It is almost comical how often the toilet seat is mentioned as a major source of irritation among women. Among men, their partner's nagging is a big source of irritation.

I see only love I see only love I see only love I see only love
I see only love **I see only love** I see only love I see only love
I see only love I see only love I see only love I see only love
I see only love I see only love I see only love I see only love
I see only love I see only love I see only love I see only love
I see only love I see only love I see only love I see only love
I see only love I see only love I see only love I see only love
I see only love I see only love I see only love I see only love
I see only love I see only love I see only love I see only love
I see only love I see only love I see only love I see only love
I see only love I see only love I see only love I see only love
I see only love I see only love **I see only love** I see only love
I see only love I see only love I see only love I see only love
I see only love I see only love I see only love I see only love
I see only love I see only love I see only love I see only love
I see only love I see only love I see only love I see only love
I see only love **I see only love** I see only love I see only love
I see only love I see only love I see only love I see only love
I see only love I see only love I see only love I see only love
I see only love I see only love I see only love I see only love
I see only love I see only love I see only love **I see only love**
I see only love I see only love I see only love I see only love
I see only love I see only love I see only love I see only love
I see only love I see only love I see only love I see only love
I see only love I see only love I see only love I see only love
I see only love I see only love I see only love I see only love
I see only love I see only love I see only love I see only love
I see only love I see only love I see only love I see only love
I see only love I see only love I see only love I see only love
I see only love I see only love I see only love I see only love
I see only love I see only love **I see only love** I see only love
I see only love I see only love I see only love I see only love
I see only love I see only love I see only love I see only love
I see only love I see only love I see only love I see only love
I see only love I see only love I see only love I see only love

Chapter 4

FINDING YOUR LOVING POWER

If we are to live more consciously, or know our-
selves more fully, or wake up from the nightmare of
our personal or collective past, it is essential to
look at the nature of our mind—how it shapes our
reality and how it might also set us free.
—JOHN WELWOOD[1]

L et me now introduce you to one of my favorite Higher
Purpose exercises, which will help you move from a position
of fear and anger to one of power and love. In terms of creating a
beautiful relationship, it has worked for me like no other and I
trust it will do the same for you.

Those of you who know my work are already familiar with
this exercise, as I have used it in prior books and in a number of
different contexts. I would like to expand upon it now, as it is an
exercise that will definitely make a positive difference in your
relationship. And what is this life-changing exercise?

PICK UP THE MIRROR INSTEAD
OF THE MAGNIFYING GLASS.

Let me explain the mirror and the magnifying glass as I am using them here:

The magnifying glass represents our symbolically pointing a finger and blaming our mate for our unhappiness. When we blame our mate we, by definition, add to the negativity that lies within the relationship. We also feel helpless, because when we think our happiness depends on someone else, we give away all our power. So not only does our relationship suffer, we personally suffer as well.

The mirror is our antidote to blame. It represents our looking inward and taking responsibility not only for our actions but also for our REACTIONS to what is going on in the relationship. When we pick up the mirror, we look not at what our mate is doing but at what we are doing— or not doing—to make ourselves unhappy. Ultimately, it is by looking into the mirror that we are able to pick up our power and discover what we personally need to do in order to change what isn't working. The mirror is our key to controlling our own happiness. Powerful indeed!

I was recently teaching a young woman the "pick up the mirror" concept. The first thing out of her mouth was, "If anybody needs to pick up the mirror, it's my husband." Hmm. I don't think she understood the concept of the mirror! It is a *guarantee* that throwing the blame and responsibility at our mate doesn't solve any relationship issues. Remember that our Higher Purpose in the relationship is to teach *ourselves* how to become more loving people. And the mirror is the perfect tool to help us to do that. I love what Marcel Proust had to say:

"The real voyage of discovery consists not in seeking new landscapes, but in having new eyes."

Your mirror will definitely give you new eyes!

By the way, if your new eyes tell you that it is your own fear, insecurity, lack of appreciation and the like that have created some or many of the difficulties in your relationship, *there is no reason to blame yourself.* Nor should you blame yourself if you don't have a relationship. For your own peace of mind, remember that we are all doing the best we can and there is *always* room for improvement. You are looking in the mirror solely for the purposes of learning and growing. Understand that:

Self-awareness is the first step toward positive change.

And your mirror is your primary tool for creating self-awareness. It removes all your denial and allows you to become honest with yourself. Looking inward, you are able to discover what you can do to keep love alive; looking outward, you won't find the answers you are seeking. Your mirror does many other things as well:

It gives you direction in terms of what actions you need to take in order to create a more loving energy, thus helping your relationship work.

It helps move you from the Lower Self, the weakest part of who you are, to the Higher Self, the most powerful and loving part of who you are. I doubt that any of you reading this book want to stay stuck in the weakest part of who you are!

When you pick up the mirror, you pick up your power. When you feel more powerful, your anger, pain and fear are diminished. When you feel more powerful, you act with integrity, compassion, caring, respect and kindness. When you pick up the mirror, you ultimately are able to find the healing light that shines within your being.

And there is a hidden benefit of the mirror: If you have issues in your relationship, you most likely have issues in other aspects of your life. So, as you use your mirror to work on healing your relationship, it will heal other aspects of your life as well.

Maybe you won't like what you initially see in the mirror. (I certainly didn't!) I beg you to put aside your judgment. I repeat:

The mirror is not an instrument for self-blame; it is an instrument of self-awareness and ultimate healing.

The mirror is there to show you the road to the best of who you are. It is there to help you recognize what you are doing to damage your relationship and to move you toward the pathway to healing your inner hurts. It shows you when the negative past is leaking into your heart and messing up the present. It points out habitual responses that get in the way of love. As you change these negative habits, you open the door to love. Wow! The mirror is a truly amazing tool!

Throughout our lives, our relationships stir up many issues about power, control, fear of betrayal and the like. "Stuff" always tries to get in the way of our loving ourselves—and our mate. But with our trusty mirror, we can always catch any problem before it gets out of hand.

Can the mirror save all relationships? Of course not. But even if the relationship ends, the rewards that come from looking into the mirror are always great. Here's an example: Carole was embroiled in a relationship in which her mate constantly pulled her down. In the beginning, whenever he criticized her, she reacted in a very angry way. In fact, she slapped his face in one of her out-of-control moments. That's a definite no-no! Luckily, he didn't slap her back. Carole was urged by all her friends to let go of the relationship, but she was having a difficult time doing so.

When she spoke to me about the situation, I suggested that until she was ready to leave, she should use the situation as an opportunity to get to the bottom of, *not his putdowns*, but her own inappropriate *reactions* to his putdowns. Yes, he was a jerk for putting her down, no doubt about it. But her intense anger was not okay. No doubt about that either. I then showed Carole the power of the mirror. I told her that instead of being so angry at his criticism, she should ask herself the question, "Why do I get so upset when he criticizes me?"

After some resistance, the light bulb finally went on inside of Carole's head. She decided to look within to get to the root of it all. Little by little, as she looked in the mirror instead of the magnifying glass, she saw, among other things:

- her need for approval,
- her deep insecurity,
- her need to be right.

Yes, she saw what it was that got in the way of her responding appropriately to her partner's constant criticism. As she worked on these various issues, she noticed that her anger began to lessen.

Carole finally reached the point where she could respond to her partner's criticism without emotional outbursts but with some version of, "I'm sorry you feel that way. I'm really comfortable with my behavior." End of story. No argument. No defensiveness. Just a "thank you for sharing, but I don't agree" kind of reaction. Her emotional attachment to his criticisms was broken.

What was even more remarkable was that as Carole looked at her own pain, she realized that her partner, too, must be in pain in order to behave so hurtfully. He, too, must be feeling insecure, weak and in need of approval. *Her anger disappeared and her compassion came forward.*

It took her a little while, but Carole finally was ready to leave the relationship. She left with love and a silent "thank you" to her former partner for his being the "practice person" in whose presence she had learned how better to love and respect herself. Lesson learned; she wouldn't have to repeat this scenario again. And she never did. Today she is happily married to a very respectful and loving man.

Let me now give you an example of how the mirror changed my life: I left so many relationships between my two marriages that it became a running joke among my friends. More accurately, they got very bored with my going in and out of relationships.

> Susan: I broke up with Bob.
> Friend: (yawning) So what else is new?

One day I asked myself, "Susan, why are you always walking out of relationships?" The magnifying glass could always come up with a fatal flaw: He was always late. Or I didn't like the way he ate. Or the way he dressed. Or his line of work. Or that he liked to play golf. Or whatever other stupid thing I could come up with. But, finally, I woke up and realized that they couldn't all be that bad; in fact, most of them were really nice people. Could it be that they were not the problem? Could it be that, horrors of horrors, *I was the problem?*

I then *forced* myself to pick up the mirror and take a long, hard look at myself. I finally faced the truth: Unless I stayed in a relationship and worked through what was going on within me, I would just keep leaving relationships for the rest of my life ... and usually for all the wrong reasons. Not good! Each time I ended a relationship, I lost my "practice person." I lost the opportunity to pick up the mirror and discover why I was so insecure.

Ultimately, I met Mark. And I *consciously* made the decision to stay put when the recurring desire to leave came upon me. I was determined to pick up the mirror and learn what I was avoiding by always leaving my relationships. It didn't take me long to figure it out. What was I avoiding? I was avoiding my fear of losing the strength I had gained by being on my own; I was avoiding my inappropriate expectations; I was avoiding my deep insecurity; I was avoiding my fear of being left; I was avoiding my need to be right—and a few other things that got in the way of love. By staying in the relationship and picking up the mirror, I was able to push through my fears and finally learn what real love was all about. Now, many years later, I am so happy I made the decision to stay.

During those earlier times when I flitted from relationship to relationship, I noticed other men and women flitting as well. And still today I notice many men and women walking out of relationships instead of looking at the truth of what is going on inside their heads and hearts. Instead of using the relationship to help them learn the secrets of loving, they take their issues with them, only to face the same situation over and over again.

Of course, this is not true of all men and women. Mark and I went out to dinner with a lovely young woman the other night. We started talking about relationships, and she told us that she was in her second marriage and was experiencing some problems. But during the entire evening she did not once blame her husband. Instead, she expressed a deep curiosity as to why she seemed to pick men who brought up the same issues for her. She realized she still had a lot to learn.

She didn't know if the marriage would last, but she felt that it was a good opportunity for figuring out what issues she still needed to work on within herself that would ultimately assure a loving relationship, either with this man or another one. Can you see the "pick up the mirror" process in action? It's like a wonderful mystery unfolding. In the end, it saves a lot of time and aggravation in our quest for a beautiful love.

So to save you time and aggravation, I suggest you begin picking up the mirror right now. Don't waste another second. The mirror allows you to remain conscious. When we blame others, we are unconscious. We are needy for control and we are traveling down the wrong path to find it. When we look in the mirror, we confront our neediness and discover that the ultimate source of control lies within our being.

Here are just a few examples of how the mirror is a great improvement over the magnifying glass as it relates to only one emotion—anger—and how it moves us to the most loving part of who we are:

The magnifying glass: I am angry he is not making more money.
The mirror: Why am I blaming him for not making more money? He's trying so hard. It's my own fear that is stopping me from creating money all by myself. I have to work on my fears.

The magnifying glass: I am angry to come home and not find my dinner waiting for me.
The mirror: I'm a spoiled brat. She is just as busy as I am. Why am I not sharing the load? I have to work on my self-ishness.

The magnifying glass: I am angry he comes home from work and just sits on the couch instead of taking over the care of the baby. I'm with that screaming child all day long!
The mirror: Why am I expecting him to take care of the baby when he comes home? He also works hard all day long. I have to take responsibility for getting some help so I will be less exhausted at night, and we can begin enjoying one another again.

The magnifying glass: I am angry because of her taking time away from me to spend time with her friends.
The mirror: Is my life so limited that I can't function without her for a few hours? It's time for me to take

responsibility to create more balance in my life so that I don't feel empty and needy when she is not around. It's actually nice that she has such great friends to hang out with. I'll have to widen my own circle of friends.

The mirror shows us how to take responsibility for creating a win-win situation. And in those cases where it is better that the relationship ends, the mirror points out the work that we need to do for ourselves to correct the situation. For example:

The magnifying glass: Why won't he stop doing drugs?
The mirror: Why do I remain with someone who is hurting himself and the relationship and refuses to go for help? I have to push through my fear of leaving.

Sometimes it's good to move on. And it does require that we push through whatever fears we have about leaving (more about that in the Addendum). But even as we leave, we have to remember to take the mirror with us. It's meant to be used for a lifetime as we encounter troubling new situations in love—and in life. It is important to remember:

The same feelings come up in a good relationship as in a bad relationship. The difference is that in a good relationship, we use the feelings as tools of self-discovery; in a bad relationship, we use the feelings to punish our mate.

In a good relationship, we pick up the mirror and ask ourselves questions such as, "What am I not doing for myself that I am expecting him/her to do for me?" In the beginning, this is a very confusing question. But as you keep asking it of yourself, you will get some very interesting answers. Remember that the smallest changes, step by step, day by day, will make a huge difference as time goes by.

Yes, even the best of relationships have their ups and downs. There is no such thing as a steady course when it comes to love. Life happens. Situations change. New issues are constantly rocking the boat of love. A great relationship is a never-ending process of:

> off course/correct,
> off-course/correct,
> off-course/correct.

We are all lovers-in-training. And as we keep picking up the mirror and correcting ourselves at those times we find ourselves off-course, our relationships (and our lives) keep getting better and better and better.

Finding and keeping love just requires that we learn the truths of love and take action based on what we have learned. Yes, it may seem unfamiliar in the beginning; after all, it takes time to break bad habits when it comes to love. But, little-by-little, we can get it right. Maybe we can learn another time, *but why not begin the journey toward love right now?*

As with most things of the heart, learning about love is a life-long process, whatever our situation. Those who have learned—*and remember to use*—the various concepts and tools that lead to harmony, caring and love are at a distinct advantage. In times of difficulty, they somehow find a way to open their hearts instead of pushing love out of their hearts. Many of these concepts and tools can be found throughout this book. *Your task is to remember to use them when difficulties arise in your own relationship.* Using your relationship—or lack of one—to learn how to become a more powerful and loving person is a truly exciting adventure. Why would anyone resist?

So I invite all of you who are reading this book to use your relationship—or lack of one—as a way of pushing through the obstacles that prevent a beautiful love from happening. And I also invite you to truly appreciate the value of that symbolic mirror, which allows you to come face-to-face with the negative habits and blind spots that make lasting love an impossibility. The mirror will allow you to develop a wide and healthy range of actions and reactions so that love can grow ... and grow ... and grow. Beautiful!

LOVE LESSONS

1) *Notice your resistances.* Awareness is an important first step. If you are having a difficult time picking up the mirror, notice your need to be right and your resistance to yielding to the idea that you may have something to do with the problems in your relationship. It is hard to take responsibility and easy to stick to the belief that it's all the fault of your mate. But it is essential for your own emotional health that you take responsibility for what you need to work on within yourself.

Not taking responsibility creates a dynamic in which one person's behavior triggers another person's behavior, which creates a vicious cycle of:

> upset and blame,
> upset and blame,
> upset and blame.

It is so much better to learn how to create a beautiful cycle of:

> caring and closeness,
> caring and closeness,
> caring and closeness.

We all have the power to do our part in creating this beautiful cycle of love.

2) *See if you can go one day without blaming your mate for anything.* Is that too long? If it is, try thirty minutes! Ten minutes? And slowly work your way up to a life time of little or no blame. When the desire to blame comes up, bite your tongue (as my mother used to say). Pick up the mirror and ask yourself, "How can I change my reaction to what is happening? How can I take more control over my life?" Blaming is counterproductive and a signal that we are not controlling our reactions. Weak! Weak!

56

Weak! So keep taking responsibility for your reactions and create a powerful and loving way of handling all that is happening in your relationship.

3) ***Become the observer of your thoughts.*** With the help of your mirror, begin to notice your thoughts so that over there is you … and over here is you watching you! In so doing, you are moving yourself one step away from the emotions that may be running you at any moment in time. This allows you to be more objective in terms of what you are doing either to help or hurt your relationship.

If your mirror tells you that your heart is controlling your thoughts, you are in a healthy space relative to love. Of course, there is always more to learn. If your mirror tells you that fear is controlling your thoughts, not to worry. It's simply time to gather and use the tools that help you to push through the fear and that ultimately allow a beautiful love to emerge. Remember not to judge yourself. Just become the observer of your thoughts and soon you will be able to move them into a more positive realm.

4) ***Keep track of your growth.*** When you have learned how to become the observer of your thoughts, you can take this a step further: Every once in a while, jot your thoughts down in your notebook and date them. At a later time, you will be able to look over your notes and notice the increased amount of love contained in your thoughts. Too often we don't notice our growth. It is only when we can look back and see where we once were that we are able to see how far we have come.

I am powerful and loving and I have nothing to fear I am powerful and loving and I have nothing to fear I am powerful and loving and I have nothing to fear I am powerful and loving and I have nothing to fear I am powerful and loving and I have nothing to fear I am powerful and loving and I have nothing to fear I am powerful and loving and I have nothing to fear I am powerful and loving and I have nothing to fear I am powerful and loving and I have nothing to fear I am powerful and loving and I have nothing to fear **I am powerful and loving and I have nothing to fear** I am powerful and loving and I have nothing to fear I am powerful and loving and I have nothing to fear I am powerful and loving and I have nothing to fear I am powerful and loving and I have nothing to fear I am powerful and loving and I have nothing to fear I am powerful and loving and I have nothing to fear I am powerful and loving and I have nothing to fear I am powerful and loving and I have nothing to fear **I am powerful and loving and I have nothing to fear** I am powerful and loving and I have nothing to fear I am powerful and loving and I have nothing to fear I am powerful and loving and I have nothing to fear I am powerful and loving and I have nothing to fear I am powerful and loving and I have nothing to fear I am powerful and loving and I have nothing to fear I am powerful and loving and I have nothing to fear I am powerful and loving and I have nothing to fear **I am powerful and loving and I have nothing to fear** I am powerful and loving and I have nothing to fear I am powerful and loving and I have nothing to fear I am powerful and loving and I have nothing to fear I am powerful and loving and I have nothing to fear I am powerful and loving and I have nothing to

Chapter 5

OUT OF NEEDINESS AND INTO LOVE

There is no love without power and there is no power without love. The greatest achievement is for us to weave power and love together as a way of life.

—SUSAN JEFFERS

I talked earlier about the concepts of selfish love and real love. As I explained, each is a product of different parts of our being. Selfish love is a product of the Lower Self, while real love is a product of the Higher Self. The differences are dramatic:

When living in the arena of the Lower Self, we are fearful; we are numb to the feelings of our mates; we don't trust our ability to carry on if something were to go wrong in our relationship; we can't truly love our mate because we are too needy and grasping. The result? Selfishness, jealousy, anger, resentment, put-downs and the like.

When living in the arena of the Higher Self, we are in the most powerful and loving part of who we are. We are self-confident; we care deeply about the feelings of our mate; we know we have the strength to handle whatever happens in the relationship; we feel complete and truly are able to love with no feeling of threat. The result? Generosity, confidence, kindness, appreciation, caring, joy and the like.

As you can see, there is a HUGE difference between the two. It is important to note that most of us tend to move back and forth between the Lower and the Higher Self depending on what is happening in our lives at any given time. Sometimes we are insecure (a Lower Self emotion); sometimes we are very confident and loving (Higher Self emotions). Our goal is to live in the arena of the Higher Self for longer and longer periods of time. This requires that we remain aware and that we keep our Higher Self "tool box" by our side so that when we notice we are acting in an unloving way—either to our mate or to ourselves—we open the tool box and use the tools (Love Lessons) that help us move into Higher Self territory once again.

So right now, take a good look and ask yourself the very telling question: "In terms of my relationship, is my mind controlled by Lower Self thinking or Higher Self thinking?" Here's a little quiz to help you decide:

- Am I using my relationship to fulfill my Higher Purpose, that of becoming a more loving person, or am I using it to blame my mate for all that is wrong in the relationship? (The latter, of course, is Lower Self thinking.)

- Do I try to control my partner or do I allow myself to be controlled? (Both imply Lower Self thinking.)

- Do I help my partner to grow as a human being or do I in any way try to stop him/her? (The latter is a sure sign of Lower Self thinking.)

- Do I depend on my partner to make me feel whole ... to make me feel secure ... to cure my loneliness? (Lower Self thinking indeed!) Or do I know that it is up to me to make myself feel whole ... secure ... and connected to the world around me. (You are in the realm of the Higher Self.)

- Do I say "thank you" frequently for all the good things that I derive from this relationship? (If you don't thank your mate for the big and little things he/she does for you, you are definitely living in the arena of the Lower Self.) Of course, if there is nothing to say thank you for (which is very rare), then why are you there? (This is a Lower Self sign that you are too frightened to leave.)

- Do I demand that everything has to be done my way or am I flexible? (The Lower Self is very rigid; the Higher Self is more relaxed, knowing you can learn and grow from everything.)

- Am I open to new ideas or do I always have to be right? (If it is the latter, the Lower Self rules!)

- Do I have an inner knowing that I can totally take care of myself, financially and emotionally, or do I need my mate for financial or emotional survival? (The inner knowing that you can take care of yourself helps you to think with a Higher Self mind. Otherwise, the Lower Self once again rules!)

You get the picture. You can also tell if you are living in the Lower or Higher Self simply by listening to what the voice inside your head is telling you. If you are hearing negative things, you know you are in the realm of the Lower Self. If you are hearing calm, loving, giving, caring and other positive thoughts, you know you are in the realm of the Higher Self. It helps to keep what I've dubbed "the Higher Self mantra" in mind at all times:

It's all happening perfectly. Whatever happens in my life, I'll handle it. I'll learn from it. I'll grow from it. I'll make it a triumph!

Very reassuring … and also very true. The reality is that within you lies a magnificent strength that truly can handle it all. Trust me on this one!

It is quite obvious that it is virtually impossible to create real love when we are stuck in the thinking of the Lower Self, the weakest and therefore the most needy part of who we are. As far as I am concerned:

NEEDINESS IS A PRIME DESTROYER OF LOVE.

Neediness is an emotion created by fear, which causes us to protect ourselves at all costs. It creates child-like behavior that is often demanding and unreasonable. It creates insecurity, which results in jealousy, anger, numbness to our partner's feelings and so on. The Lower Self in action: Not good for relationships!

It stands to reason that if we are feeling needy, consciously or unconsciously, we will try to manipulate our mate in the desperate hope that they will fill our needs. The needy child rules our being, and between you and me, *a child cannot experience real love, whether they are 8 or 81.* We truly have to grow up in order to create a loving relationship. The good news is that:

The minute that we grow up, the minute that we connect to the part of us that is strong, confident and giving, the entire nature of the relationship changes. It is then that real love is possible.

Read that again. I believe that without embracing the best of who we are, our Higher Self, we will always be filled with a deep fear and emptiness that our mate can never fill. And problems ensue.

Ben and Jenna offer a perfect example. For six years, Jenna was a stay-at-home mother. An actress prior to their marriage, she gave up her career to raise their son, who now was going to school full-time. Her days had become empty and unfulfilling. She missed her acting career. In addition, her confidence had diminished greatly as a result of being home for so many years. Jenna felt that while she had gained a treasured son, she had lost an important part of herself.

Then, through an unexpected set of circumstances, and much to her amazement and delight, she was offered a part in a television series. It was a small part, but it was a welcome opportunity to restart her career. She couldn't wait to tell Ben the good news. But instead of the congratulations and delight she expected, Ben strongly objected, insisting that he wanted her to stay at home. He came up with a lot of "logical" reasons why she shouldn't work, but, in truth, he was threatened by her moving out into the world, meeting new people, earning her own money. In other words, he was threatened by her growing independence. Many fights ensued. Despite Ben's objections, Jenna accepted the job, knowing that it was something important for her own sense of well-being.

As Jenna had hoped, her work caused her confidence to soar. She was gaining back an important part of herself, which she had sorely missed as a full-time parent. At the same time, Ben's comfort diminished, as he felt he was losing control of Jenna. Unfortunately, Ben, the person who *claimed* to love Jenna, became her biggest critic. The put-downs began and from then on never stopped. Although he didn't lie on the floor and have a tantrum, his behavior was as irrational as a child's often is. "I want it my way!" Jenna became angry and defensive, not understanding why Ben was so unsupportive when her work was making her so happy. Neither of them could see that Ben's insecurity was running his emotions and ultimately ruining the relationship.

Eventually the marriage ended. Even as he moved out of the house, Ben's feeling was that, "It's all her fault that the marriage ended." Ben was living in his Lower Self, which explains why he couldn't look into the mirror and see that he was responsible for the mess in his life. But he really was. And if he had moved into his Higher Self, he would have picked up the mirror and listened to his Higher Self mantra, which would have told him:

"Ben, don't worry. It's all happening perfectly. Whatever happens in your life, you'll handle it. You'll learn from it. You'll grow from it. You'll make it a triumph!"

And the outcome would have been very different. Two marriages later, Ben figured it all out.

Patsy and Tom experienced a similar situation. Tom wanted to go into partnership with a friend to start a property venture that was very exciting to him. Patsy wanted only the steady income of his job. Her insecurity about money made her unsympathetic relative to Tom's feelings of boredom and lack of fulfillment in his present job. She wanted it to be her way. Much to her dismay, Tom followed his heart.

It took a few years for the new venture to become profitable, but eventually, it was successful. However, his marriage fell apart. Patsy never was able to support Tom in his goals. She was angry and judgmental from the start, and ultimately he left. To this day, Patsy complains about her ex. If she had picked up the mirror instead of the magnifying glass, she would have realized that she created her own unhappiness by not facing her fears about money and finding a creative solution to her concerns. She never understood that *HER fears should not ruin HIS life*. I don't think she ever figured it out. She's still angry.

Certainly an important sign of a Higher Self love is that we support our partner's growth. If both Ben and Patsy had understood the concept of picking up the mirror instead of the magnifying glass, they quickly would have seen their own deep insecurity. Ironically, they were afraid that their mate's actions would ruin their relationships, yet they were wrong: *It was their insecurity that ruined—and ultimately ended—their relationships.* Psychiatrist David Viscott was right on target when he said:

> "The surest way to destroy a relationship is for one partner to stand in the way of the other partner's self-fulfillment. If you think about it, that goes against everything a relationship stands for. A partner should be able to rely on the other's love and support to help him grow into the person he feels destined to be. To stand in the way is the same as saying, 'I don't want you to be yourself.'"[1]

To stand in someone's way is also the same as saying, "I'm incapable of loving you because my own insecurities are getting in the way." You'll recognize this as selfish love in action. Remember that:

As we support each other in growing, love can't help but grow as well.

You might be asking, "Susan, why couldn't Jenna have stayed at home to please Ben? Wouldn't that have been a loving thing to do?" Or, "Why couldn't Tom just have stayed in his job to please Patsy?" Good and fair questions … and there certainly are times when it is appropriate and loving to do things just to please our mate … but *when it comes to our own sense of personal fulfillment it is important that we follow our own path of growth and that we support our mate in doing the same.* (I will talk more about this later.)

When we are in a relationship, it is always important to honor the truth of who we are. *We can't allow ourselves to become victims of our mate's insecurities.* If we are afraid of doing what is right for us because it will upset our mate, this is simply another form of Lower Self thinking. Inevitably we will feel resentful of our mate, even though if we picked up our mirror we would see that the problem wasn't our mate's objection; the problem was that we failed to take responsibility for our own life. It's very tricky, isn't it? But it is clear to me that two healthy people in a relationship want to support each other's growth. We may have a twinge of fear as our mate begins to spread his/her wings, but as we cheer each other on, a deep closeness can grow.

Let me now tell you an interesting concept that I learned from a wonderful teacher named Ken Keyes a number of years ago. It explains a lot about irrational behavior in a relationship. And that concept is "control addictions." Keyes said that you can always tell something is an addiction if you can't let go, even if it is causing you to experience "separating emotions" such as anger, fear, resentment, jealousy and unhappiness as opposed to "unifying emotions" such as acceptance, love, joy, happiness and peace. Ideally, our goal is to learn how to let go and be more flexible and flowing. Keyes tells us that the way to do this is to *upgrade our "addictions" to "preferences."*[2]

What does that mean? It's actually quite simple. An addiction to control is very rigid: "I want it my way!" A preference is much more flexible. A preference says:

> "Yes, I prefer it this way, but I will go along with your way as I know it makes you happy. I will find a way to deal with my own issues about it."

If Ben had been able to do this, he could have said to himself:

"Yes, I like Jenna being home, but I know she is unhappy staying at home. She should have the opportunity to fulfill herself in the outside world. I'm a little bit nervous about losing her, if the truth be known, but I'll work on my insecurities. We'll make it work somehow. Isn't it exciting she got such a good job? Let's celebrate!"

Oh, Ben, why didn't you pick up the mirror!? How different it all could have been!

And how about Patsy? How might she have changed her addiction to a preference regarding her husband starting his own business? It might sound like this:

"I prefer that he stays in his job, where I feel more secure relative to money, but he has to follow his dream. I know I would resent it if I couldn't follow my dream. And who knows? He may succeed really well at it. And I can always find a way to make more money if we need it. I'll support him to the best of my ability."

With this kind of thinking, not only would she have had an opportunity to push through her fears about money and taken more control of her life, but her marriage would have become an exciting partnership instead of an angry mess.

If we can upgrade our addictions to the level of *preferences*, we are no longer resentful and unhappy. "If it's this way, that's great. If it's not this way, that's great. We'll find a way to make it work." Ken Keyes believed that upgrading all our addictions to preferences is the key technique in the science of happiness. I agree! As we transform our addictions to preferences, we notice that our buttons rarely get pressed. Peace of mind ensues. What a tonic for a relationship!

I recently had an opportunity to turn an addiction to a preference in my own life. Here's what happened: Mark and I make a point of not allowing anyone or anything to interfere with our precious weekends together. But then it happened. Mark was invited by a friend to watch the final matches in a rugby tournament that was being transmitted to our local pub by satellite, a big thing when you are British, love rugby and live in Los Angeles! The problem was that the matches took place on Saturday mornings. Since Mark loved rugby, he accepted the invitation.

Even though the rugby matches took place on just a few Saturday mornings, my buttons were pressed. I was disappointed and angry that he had accepted. After all, Saturday was OUR day! "How could he choose to go and watch rugby instead of wanting to be with me!" I must admit, he invited me to come along, but I had absolutely no desire to spend my Saturdays mornings watching rugby, a game I have no interest in. (Sorry about that, rugby fans.) Naturally, he felt my upset and gently explained that he loved rugby … and they only lasted two hours … and he hadn't had an opportunity to watch the games for years … and it wasn't every Saturday—just when the important matches were being played. This didn't stop my pouting and looks of disdain. The Lower Self in action. Yuck!

Luckily, it took me only one weekend to remember to pick up my mirror and throw away the magnifying glass. When I did, I realized that I had a "Saturday-togetherness" addiction. With this realization, my task was simple: it was to move my addiction to the level of a preference. "Yes, I would prefer that Mark were here on those Saturday mornings that he is going to watch the rugby matches. But it gives him such pleasure and I want him to have pleasure. Besides, we still have the rest of the day together. I will find a way to make it work for both of us."

I then asked my mirror, "Instead of being childishly upset, what could I do to create a happy time for myself when he was not there on those Saturday mornings?" And I came up with some very enjoyable things I could do. I could rent some videos and watch movies that I knew Mark was not interested in seeing. I could use this peaceful time to do some work on my new book. I could walk on our beautiful beach. I could have breakfast with friends. As I began to put my ideas into practice, something interesting happened: I began truly to enjoy those Saturday mornings when he went off to watch the rugby matches! What is truly significant is that my mirror made me realize that:

> It was my addiction to Saturdays being a certain way that had made me unhappy ... *not Mark's going to the rugby matches.*

A big realization! You'll notice that I went from a child-wanting-it-to-be-my-way-or-I-will-be-miserable to an adult who was clearly able to satisfy my own needs. My happiness did not depend on whether my husband went to a rugby match or not! While I love him to be with me on Saturday mornings, it is now a preference, not an addiction. Needless to say, my interaction with Mark about his rugby games was greatly altered as a result. With a sense of wholeness, I could give him a big hug and kiss when he went off to his game and honestly and joyfully wish him a wonderful time. Happiness restored!

By the way, after my upset passed, I thought about going to the rugby matches with Mark. But, out of love, I truly felt I would diminish his enjoyment of the games—a fish out of water, so to speak. He and his friends came away hoarse from screaming their team to victory ... or defeat. I just couldn't have worked up that much enthusiasm. In the end, I was able to take pleasure from his pleasure.

Whether it's something minor like my silly Saturday morning saga ... or something more serious like Ben and Patsy wanting to stop their mates from living their dreams, we have to ask ourselves if we are going to stay stuck in neediness and fear or move ourselves into a stronger and more loving place—an important step in creating a lasting relationship. This requires that we stop focusing on fixing and changing our partner; rather, we focus on fixing and changing ourselves—our mirror in action. We work on pulling ourselves out of our neediness and building our confidence enough to come together with our partners in the spirit of sharing a beautiful life. It is this kind of sharing that is the basis of real love.

You can now understand why we need to pull ourselves out of the mire of Lower Self thinking and upgrade our control addictions to preferences as Ken Keyes wisely taught us. We need to become adults in love. An adult feels secure, doesn't blame, takes responsibility for his/her experience of life, isn't rigid, goes with the flow, expects to contribute his/her fair share, keeps his/her word, appreciates and doesn't take things for granted. Yes, an adult truly is an amazing picture of power and love.

Of course, throughout life there is always the dance between being a child and being an adult. All of us, men and women alike, by virtue of the fact that we are human beings, feel insecure at times. Some of us are more self-assured than others, but we all have our vulnerable spots. Even if you are way ahead of the game and have already created a beautiful love, I am sure you will agree that there is always more to learn.

Over the years, we all develop a number of habitual ways of being that stop us from loving fully. But as we keep picking up our valuable mirror, we slowly but surely move into a more powerful and loving part of who we are. And problems in a relationship are resolved more and more quickly. Note that it only took me one Saturday to discover what was wrong about my thinking relative to Mark going to the rugby matches, and I was able to change my attitude quickly. When I was younger, my upset might have gone on indefinitely. While growing up takes practice, with each step we take, it gets easier and easier and easier. And the problems get solved faster and faster and faster.

Once you start pulling yourself out of your insecurity, it's as though a curtain begins to lift and you can see more clearly and more lovingly. Of course, if both you and your mate are able to do this together, that's great. But for now, begin with yourself. As you already learned, feelings are contagious. Perhaps your picking up the mirror will inspire your mate to pick up his/her mirror as well. It often works that way.

The bottom line is that it is important that you make moving yourself into the arena of the Higher Self, the best of who you are, one of your top priorities. There is no question in my mind that creating a lasting love ... a real love ... depends on it.

LOVE LESSONS

1) ***Don't lose yourself in a relationship; and if you are already lost, find yourself once again.*** How do you make sure not to lose yourself? This exercise, adapted from *Feel the Fear and Do It Anyway,* will get you started:[3]

a) Create a rich, balanced life for yourself so that the absence of any part of your life doesn't wipe you out. We all must be careful not to define ourselves only in terms of a relationship. Relationship has to be *one part* of a rich, glorious life. If your life is rich with friends, family, career, personal growth, contributions to the world and more, then if the relationship ends, you have a hole in your life, but you aren't wiped out. It may take a little while, but you know you will always get to the other side where happiness reigns once again.

b) As you begin filling your life with wonderful things, remember to commit 100 percent to all aspects of your life, knowing that you count:

When you are with your family, be there 100 percent, knowing that you count.

When you are at work, be there 100 percent, knowing that you count.

When you are focusing on your personal growth, be there 100 percent, knowing that you count.

When you are with friends, be there 100 percent, knowing that you count.

When you participate in the community, be there
100 percent, knowing that you count.

This means ... care, pay attention and, most crucially, realize
that you are important. You make a difference. Every action you
take affects everyone around you. Wow! If this isn't finding yourself, I don't know what is!

c) If you still don't think you are important, then act-as-if
you do. Constantly ask yourself:

If I were really important in my relationship, what
would I be doing?

If I were really important in my job, what would I
be doing?

If I were really important to my friends, what
would I be doing?

If I were really important in my community, what
would I be doing?

Make a list of what you would be doing if you were really
important ... and then go about doing it. In time, you will
actually "live into" the reality that you really are important!

In real love, we are not "attached" to our mate. Yes, we are a
team, but we are, at the same time, two whole people capable of
standing on our own. There is no question that when the heart opens
it is vulnerable. It can get wounded so easily. But when we feel
whole, when we feel strong, when we feel we are a part of it all, we
can be safely vulnerable, always knowing that no matter what happens, we will handle it all. In this way, our neediness disappears. We

are fulfilled. And our ability to love with a sense of confidence and joy radiates throughout our being. We become a magnet to all that is good in this world—and that includes a truly wonderful relationship.

*2) **Work on upgrading your control addictions to preferences.*** Everything seems to be going fine and then something our mate says or does creates a feeling of threat and/or upset. An inner, sometimes unconscious, button is being pressed that signals, "Danger. I'm losing control." Here's the plan:

a) *The minute our button is pressed, this is our cue to pick up the mirror, instead of attacking our mate.* In the beginning, we tend to forget and arguments ensue. We need to put reminders all around us that say, "Pick up the mirror!" When it comes to a difficult situation in our relationships, the sooner we can pick up the mirror, the sooner the situation will be happily resolved.

b) Our mirror tells us that we are definitely addicted to something being a certain way. Aha! We are learning something important about ourselves!

c) We then need to ask ourselves (our mirror), "What button is being pressed? Why can't I let go of my position? How do I change my addiction to control to a preference so that this can be a win-win situation?"

d) We then ask ourselves how we can turn this initial upset into something more acceptable so that our reaction becomes a preference instead of a need.

e) We put on our thinking caps and get very creative about making changes in our thinking that bring peace of mind, fulfillment and satisfaction.

You can see that this process allows us to make most situations work for both ourselves and our mates. So practice, practice, practice this mind-altering tool and your relationship will benefit immeasurably. (Note that there are times where your mate's choices in life are destructive by definition—for example, if he/she is compulsively gambling or trying to stifle your dreams. The Addendum helps you deal with such situations.)

3) *Make "the Higher Self mantra" a part of your life.* In case you have forgotten it, let me repeat the Higher Self mantra here:

It's all happening perfectly. Whatever happens in my life, I'll handle it. I'll learn from it. I'll grow from it. I'll make it a triumph!

Say it now. Say it again. And say it once more. Feel the peace that comes from this kind of thinking. As a matter of fact, write it down so you can carry it with you and when doubts come into your head, pull it out of your pocket and read it over and over again. If you keep saying it often enough, this mantra will begin roaming *automatically* through your head in good times and bad. When this happens, you are well on your way to thinking in a Higher Self way. Peace at last!

4) *Become the mate you want your mate to be.* I love this exercise. First make a list of all the characteristics you want your mate to have. It could look like this:

> loving, thoughtful, warm, considerate,
> caring, appreciative, romantic, generous

Now for the big challenge:

PICK UP THE MIRROR AND BEGIN
DEVELOPING THESE QUALITIES IN YOURSELF.

"Susan, that's sneaky!" I know. You didn't want to hear that. But how can we ask our mates to be something we have been unable or unwilling to be ourselves? Also, as you learned in Chapter 3, loving behavior is contagious! Just incorporating all these loving qualities into our own being can dramatically alter the thoughts and actions of our mate. Also, remember the Higher Purpose of your relationship ... and that is to become a more loving person. This is a perfect opportunity to do so. The questions you need to ask yourself are:

> How can I become more loving?
> How can I become warmer?
> How can I become more appreciative?
> How can I become more considerate?
> How can I become more caring?
> How can I become more secure?
> How can I become more thoughtful?
> How can I become more romantic?
> How can I become more generous?

Now, using your own list, answer the questions for yourself. For example:

"I can become more loving simply by expressing my love more often. I will make "I love you" a regular part of our communication."

"I can become warmer by always giving him/her a hug before I leave the house instead of a "see you later" as I run out the door."

76

"I can become more appreciative by noticing and then saying 'thank you' for all the little things that he/she does for me."

And so on.

After answering your list of questions, you need to **TAKE ACTION**—at your own pace—to become the loving mate you would want your mate to be. Your goal? *Maximum caring and minimum need.* Powerfully loving indeed!

PART II

THE ESSENCE

Let's now get down to the nitty-gritty of handling the big and little issues that get in the way of love. There are good ways … and bad ways … to handle these issues. It's very important to know the difference!

I speak only love I speak only

Chapter 6

THE SECRETS OF LOVING
COMMUNICATION

Real compassion is a strength born of a shared
weakness, a recognition of a common humanity, a
way of healing the wounds of separation by mak-
ing connections, and it contains an acceptance of
the fact that even in their deepest being, everyone
is helpless and would welcome love from us.
                                                    —MERLE SHAIN[1]

I once was given a book with the title *Everything Men Know About Women* by Dr. Alan Francis.[2] The back cover revealed that it was "fiercely frank and brilliantly insightful" and "the most complete picture ever revealed of men's knowledge of their opposite sex." Sounded good to me! When I began flipping through the pages, I had a very good laugh—the pages were totally blank! I'm sorry there wasn't a companion book entitled *Everything Women Know About Men.* Maybe I'll write it!

While humor is wonderful, we can't overlook the seriousness of a couple unable to communicate. Health journalist Alison Rose

Levy gives us a poignant and revealing look at the lack of communication that symbolically can happen between two people, citing Eugene Ionesco's play, *The Bald Soprano:*[3]

> "Two people, seated together at a dinner party, have an extended conversation in which they gradually come to realize that they live in the same city, the same neighborhood, the same street, building, and even apartment. As each new revelation occurs, one or the other remarks upon the amazing coincidence. Ultimately, they discover that they are, in fact, husband and wife. The contrast between the presumed intimacy of marriage and the polite alienation of this clueless couple expresses with dramatic power just how far the love relationship can deviate from the ideal."

It may sound far-fetched, but in many ways Ionesco's insightful story imitates life for some couples. For example, too often I hear an anguished man or woman tell me that their mate unaccountably announced one day, "I am not happy and I am leaving. Goodbye." Their sorrowful cry is, "I didn't even know he/she was unhappy!" Our society is advanced in a lot of ways, yet too many of us are totally unable to fill the most basic of human needs—the need to share our upsets and be a source of comfort to one another. One wonders how two people can share so much of life but not the most important part … what is going on inside their hearts and minds.

I want to share with you something I wrote way back in 1972. It was shortly after the break-up of my first marriage of sixteen years and it illustrates how, in a number of ways, my ex-husband and I could have been the two characters in Ionesco's play:

We thought one got married and lived happily ever after;
We didn't know that relationships require hard work …

We thought it wasn't any good if we had to ask for what
*   we needed;*
We didn't know that no one is a mind reader ...

We thought all our needs should have been filled with
*   our marriage;*
We didn't know what our most important need was—a
*   sense of self ...*

We thought our becoming one made us whole;
We didn't know two whole people were necessary from
*   the start ...*

We thought he had to be strong and take care of her;
We didn't know we were supposed to take care of each
*   other ...*

We thought it was disloyal to grow as an individual;
We didn't know how stifling too much togetherness
*   could be ...*

We thought that when the other grew, it was a threat;
We didn't know we were good enough, and shouldn't feel
*   threatened ...*

We thought money would make us secure;
We did not know that security meant knowing you could
*   make it ... with or without money ...*

We thought those who went for help were weak;
We didn't know that everyone needs help ...

We thought the other wasn't giving;
We didn't know we weren't taking in ...

He thought I was happy;
He didn't know how frightened I was ...

I thought he was happy;
I didn't know how frightened he was ...

We didn't know ... We just didn't know ...
There was so much we didn't know ...

Yes, there was so much we didn't know. You can see from the above how important it is that we do what is necessary to learn how to communicate *lovingly* with our partner. Without good communication, loneliness fills our being. This loneliness is a contributing factor to one or both partners having affairs, finding ways to stay away from home and ultimately separating. One of my students reported that when he finally separated from his wife, he found he was less lonely than when they lived together. I know many of you reading this will understand exactly what he was talking about. Yes, when there is bad or no communication, married people can, strangely, be much lonelier than single people!

And if we have unloving thoughts as a result of our inability to communicate, the loneliness is intensified. Unloving thoughts make it a you-versus-me world instead of a "we're-both-in-it-together" world. By definition, when we are not in touch with our loving side, we widen the distance between us, making the loneliness even more pronounced.

The good news is that loneliness can be a teacher; it need not be destructive. In fact, if channeled properly, it can be constructive. Our loneliness can signal when it's time to pick up the mirror and change our behavior so that we can feel closer to our mate instead of acting as two strangers meeting in the night ... and day! In this way, we can see loneliness as a force that pushes us to tear down the walls. As we do this, our relationship has a chance of getting better and better and better, thus lessening the need to look for love outside it.

I know that men often are blamed for being the quiet ones when it comes to feelings. Certainly it seems that way, except for the fact that many of the "leavers" I describe above are women who certainly didn't tell their truth to their mates—until the day they left! I guess both men and women have a lot to learn about telling the truth *first to themselves* and then to their mates.

Certainly Mark and I had a lot to learn about communication in the beginning. When we began dating, he was quiet, quiet, quiet, and I talked, talked, talked. After a relatively short period of time, my great power of observation made me notice the disparity! I was running out of things to talk about (if you can believe that) and I was certainly learning nothing about him. This was not good for a developing relationship. What to do? I finally came up with a plan: I decided I would try keeping my mouth shut when we went out to dinner the next time, thereby leaving room for him to talk.

The evening arrived and the meal was uncomfortably silent to be sure. Finally, Mark asked if something was wrong. I explained that I realized I talked so much that I didn't leave any room for him to talk, so I thought I would shut up and give him a chance. He said he enjoyed listening to me; he found me very interesting. I said that was nice of him to say, but if he didn't talk, how could I learn anything about him. I also told him that it didn't seem fair for me to have to provide the "entertainment" for the evening. (You'll notice I was a bit sarcastic in those early days.)

I asked him why he was always so quiet. He said, "Training, I guess." He explained that that at the age of seven, he was sent back to England from Singapore (where his father was in the colonial service) to attend boarding school. It was all so new and, in the beginning, he missed his family terribly. When he expressed his feelings and cried a few tears, he was teased mercilessly and literally beaten by the older boys (which was an acceptable practice at the time). So he and all the other boys there learned at a very early age not to express their feelings.*

Aha! I had learned something about him. I suggested it was now time for him to begin sharing his feelings with me, and I also made a deal with him: I promised that if he shared his feelings, I wouldn't beat him up! I kept my promise.

Over the years, as closeness has grown between us, Mark has learned to share the heart and soul of whom he is. And I have learned not to be sarcastic and hurtful, which in the beginning, was a very bad habit of mine. You see, for many years before meeting Mark, I had a tendency toward one-upmanship (a characteristic of the Lower Self) and I was good at doing *anything* to win my case. Not a pretty picture. As I learned to communicate in a more loving way, we both felt much safer to open up to the truth of who we are.

Let me now pass along to you my Lucky 13 Love Lessons as they relate to communication. They are meant to tear down the walls and create a safe place for closeness to occur, helping you to approach your mate as a friend instead of an enemy. Keep in mind your Higher Purpose … that of becoming a more loving person. It helps to remember that it lowers our sense of self-esteem when we hurt other people. In all our interactions with our partner, we need to be responsible for what we say and do.

---

*In spite of this, Mark credits boarding school for giving him the wonderful strength he today feels. It just took a little getting used to in the beginning.

LOVE LESSONS

1) *Approach your mate with a loving energy.* Before you say a word to your mate, you've "said" a lot. Your aura is either "I love you; let's work this out" or it's "I'm angry and it's your fault." As you learned in Chapter 3, feelings are contagious. When your words come from "I love you; let's work it out," the outcome will be much more satisfactory. Also, you can communicate much more sensitive information when you come from a place of love rather than anger. Obviously, it makes sense to change your energy to the side of love before you even begin to talk about a difficult issue with your mate.

Also in Chapter 3, I showed you how to send "I love you" messages telepathically. This works wonderfully as a way of setting the stage for communication. Just silently repeat the healing words "I love you" over and over again before you speak. You may think this is ridiculous, but trust me: repeating the words "I love you" as you think about or look at your mate is a fantastic energy (aura) changer. It creates a loving space within you, which radiates to your mate. It is certainly best not to speak about any issue, especially if it is a difficult one, until you can create within yourself a loving connection with your mate.

Another way to move into a loving space is to "accentuate the positive and eliminate the negative," as the song tells us. For example, before complaining to your mate, write down five positive things about him/her to diffuse your negative thoughts. You won't be so hard on your mate as you think about the gifts he/she brings to your life.

Remember that "like attracts like." If we are angry and negative, we most likely will get an angry and negative response in return. If we are caring and positive, we most likely will get a caring and positive response in return. I trust you will choose the latter.

2) ***Be honest with yourself so you can be honest with your mate.*** Very often our "honesty" is unwittingly an untruth. We lash out at our mate for something that we need to heal within ourselves. In such a case, *our upset has nothing to do with them.* In such a case, our truth is *not* our truth!

Of course, at the time, we may not even be aware of this. So when we are angry, it is our task to learn whether there is something we are denying within ourselves. Complicated, isn't it? But with our trusty little mirror, we can learn a lot. We can ask ourselves questions such as:

"Is my upset *not* about him/her but really about:

- my worries about money?"
- how difficult it is taking care of the kids?"
- my feeling unattractive?"
- my insecurity and my needing constant assurance?"
- my boss giving me a hard time today?"
- the fact that I don't appreciate all the good my mate does for me?"
- my unreasonable expectations?"
- the fact that I am blaming and not taking responsibility for my life?"

And so on. As we pick up the mirror, we may notice many things we need to handle within ourselves that have nothing to do with our mate.

Interestingly, once we have figured out the truth of why we are so upset, we usually do not feel the same negativity toward our mate anymore. Therefore:

Had we told him/her the "truth" before we worked it out within our mind, we would have been telling a "lie."

Oh, our minds are so complicated! You can see that if we can push through the lies we tell ourselves, we usually get to the heart of the matter. We take responsibility for our actions and reactions and end up on the side of love. Too often, our "I'm just being honest" is an excuse for an unwarranted attack on our mate. So, just to reinforce this important reality:

> When you are feeling negative toward your mate, it's not a great time to tell him/her. It's time to pick up the mirror instead of the magnifying glass and get to the truth of why you are upset. By being truthful to yourself, you get to the heart—and hurt—of the matter. And you can proceed to talk to your mate in a much more loving and responsible voice.

In my first marriage, I never was able to take responsibility for the anger I was feeling. Then came the day the volcano exploded. When I got in touch with my anger, I couldn't turn it off. Nor could I put it to good use. I didn't know how to pick up the mirror and take responsibility for what was happening in my life. In the process, my heart totally closed and it truly was the end of the relationship.

So it is essential that we use our anger to learn more about who we are, what we need, and what we must do to change what is not working in our lives. The quality of our relationships—and our lives—depends on it.

3) *Anger needs expression ... in a loving way.* Sometimes our mate's behavior makes us want to scream with anger. And, indeed, none of us should in any way be the proverbial doormat. But, even if our anger is justified, we have to be aware of how badly we can hurt our mates when we attack them with vicious words. I might add that regrettably it is impossible to take back hurtful words spoken in anger.

It helps to keep in mind that when our mate behaves badly, it is usually their own pain, or insecurity, or ignorance of our feelings that is causing his/her awful behavior. This requires that we develop a sense of compassion. Compassion comes from the understanding we all have our weaknesses. There are no exceptions, including ourselves!

With compassion in hand, it is important that we let our mate know that he/she is doing something that is a no-no for us. It is important that our mate understands how his/her actions are making us feel. But we express our upset lovingly. Yes, you can rant and rage, but it is doubtful that this kind of behavior will create closeness in a relationship!

How can we best approach our mate about something that is clearly not okay with us? First we get a deep clarity within. Clarity is essential, otherwise our mate probably won't understand that this is important to us. When we approach our mate with the strength of our clarity, it sounds something like this:

> "Helen, I know you are just having fun, but it is not okay with me that you joke about me in front of our friends. I don't think it's funny; in fact, it hurts me very deeply. I know you love me and don't want to hurt me, so please stop the joking. It would mean a lot to me."

If certain behavior is not okay with us and we express it clearly and without blame, we are playing our part in helping to eradicate situations that take away love. Your mate may not have understood that they were doing something that is hurtful to you. Hopefully, they will see the error of their ways and stop their hurtful behavior. If not … well … I'll talk about that in the Addendum.

A few words about our own behavior: The sound of love does not include nagging, a trait attributed, perhaps unfairly, to women. Certainly many men nag as well. In any case, if you want to keep love alive, the nagging simply has to go. It is reported that many men work late hours to avoid the nagging they will face when they walk in the door. Maybe that's true; maybe it isn't. But listen to what self-improvement pioneer Dale Carnegie has to say about why dogs are so popular: "THEY GO CRAZY WITH EXCITE-MENT EVERY TIME THEY SEE YOU."[4] Take a lesson. If, instead of nagging, you go crazy with love and excitement when your mate walks in the door, I suspect he/she will try very hard to get home early! To be fair, perhaps his/her job makes this impossible, but he/she will feel blessed knowing you are there to welcome him/her home.

Neither does the sound of love include teasing. Sometimes teasing seems harmless and silly and fun, but it is unhealthy and often hurtful. I remember a time when two happy newlyweds came to visit. It soon became apparent that one of their ways of being "endearing" to one another was to tease each other regarding various personality traits. I said to them, "Don't do that to each other." They were surprised and said, "We just do it in fun." I replied, "Yes, and one day when you are angry about something, it won't seem so funny anymore and you will have started on the downhill slope. It's not a good thing to do if you are interested in creating a beautiful love!" It's one thing to make fun of yourself (I make fun of myself all the time), but to make fun of the other isn't acceptable in a loving relationship.

At the very beginning of our relationship, Mark tried teasing me a few times when we were out with friends. When we were alone, I explained to him very clearly that that was a no-no. I also threatened to embarrass him mercilessly if he ever did it again! Not a loving response (and I wouldn't do that today, knowing what I have learned over the years), but, thankfully, he heard me and apologized. And the good news is that he never did it again. And thus began our "habit" of saying only loving and caring things to each other ... and about each other. We have been very successful at that. So no more teasing. Only loving words are allowed!

4) *Speak to the light within your mate.* When my daughter, Leslie, was in her early twenties, we were having great difficulty communicating. She made the decision that we needed a mediator.

(Oh, the wisdom of the young ... sometimes!) I told her to find one and, much to my delight, she did. She found a lovely spiritual woman, Guru Darshan, who knew just what to do to make us listen to each other and actually hear what the other was saying.

She sat us both down and put a candle between us. She said that during the session, we were to speak to each other, but look only at the light as we spoke, the light representing the beauty and love within that may at times be dimmed by the difficulties of life itself. Leslie was to tell me what was on her mind. I was to listen, with no interruptions, until she had finished. I then was to repeat what I *thought* she had said. If Leslie agreed that I understood what she said, then it was my turn. I was to look at the light and tell her what was on my mind. She was not allowed to interrupt me until I had finished. She then repeated what she *thought* I had said. If I agreed that she understood what I had said, then it was her turn once again. This back and forth process continued for four hours. (We obviously had a lot to say and understand.) It was magical.

As powerful as hearing and understanding what the other was saying was that candle, a symbol of the light within. Sometimes circumstances in life dim the light within and make us act in very hurtful ways. And sometimes circumstances in life dim the light in those we love. The candle is a symbol of the beauty that, even when covered by pain, hurt, fear and other negative things, is always there.

This is a very effective exercise for helping us get in touch with the suffering in ourselves and in our mate, and it helps us to have compassion. It is listening in a spiritual way ... listening from the best of who we are. It's not about who's right and who's wrong, but simply about how each one of us feels. It's the beginning of our healing a hurtful situation. To this day, many years later, when Leslie acts in a way that bothers me, I see the light. I know that when I act in a way that bothers her, she sees the light as well. Our relationship is now loving, patient and kind.

I have tried very hard, and thankfully with great success, to apply the same technique when I am talking to anyone, especially my husband, Mark. Of course, at times, I forget about the light and my own insecurities get in the way, but I am quick to remind myself about it and move over to the side of love. There is something almost magical about that process. What I am doing is simply shifting from the Lower Self to the Higher Self—from the worst of who I am to the best. Actually, it isn't magic at all; it's just a wonderful and wise choice.

5) *Remember that you may be right ... or you may be wrong.* Sometimes our anger is about our perception of a situation. When we are angry about something, it is best to approach it not as right or wrong, but as "this is how it feels to me." In such cases (actually in all cases) it is better not to blame but to take responsibility for our upset. For example, if you feel your mate is driving too fast, it's not:

"Pull back! You're driving much too close to the car in front of you!"

In this case, you are casting blame, but who is right and who is wrong? Obviously your mate is comfortable with the situation. The reality is simply that the situation is making you uncomfortable. A more effective and accurate communication is:

"Darling, I get nervous when we are so close to the car in front of us. It would make me more comfortable if you pulled back a bit."*

This response isn't about right and wrong, but simply about your own comfort. Maybe he/she will pull back, maybe not. (It works for me.) But at least, you've approached the situation in a loving manner, and one that doesn't make your mate wrong.

_____

*I suggest you use terms of endearment—Honey, Sweetheart or whatever works for you—to pave the way for a loving connection instead of a heated argument.

Always remember that blaming is never an effective way to communicate. It's important to take responsibility for our feelings, actions and words. Only in that way can honest, clear communication take place. I can hear a lot of "yeah, buts" out there. I know this isn't easy, but in terms of our needs and our mate's needs, we have to get very creative in telling our truth without hurting our mate.

6) *Override your negativity and "lie" lovingly.* You are irrationally upset. You know your upset is irrational. With clenched teeth, if need be, let what comes from your mouth be loving, *even if you are not feeling loving.* This means saying something good instead of something bad even though you are tempted to say something bad. For example, you sit down to dinner together and you want to complain about the fact that he/she was late coming home from work. Knowing your mate is in the middle of a lot of pressure at work at the moment, it would be irrational and punishing to say, "It really makes me angry that you came home late today." Instead, clench your teeth and say, "I'm so happy when we are together. I love you."

You most likely will get a loving response back. He/she will be happy to be at home with you. And the miracle of such an approach is that *your own tension will melt and you will feel the beauty of the moment instead of being the one to destroy it.* Yes, sometimes it's best not to reveal our unjustified upset and, instead, tell a loving lie. It's a very beautiful thing to do.

7) *Let your partner know what you need.* In one of my workshops, a woman judgmentally announced, "If I have to tell him what I need, then he mustn't care that much." My answer was a loud, *"Of course you have to tell him what you need; he's not a mind-reader!"* Yes, some men and women are more intuitive than others, but regardless, *just to be sure*, we have to tell our mate what it is that we need! Maybe if you tell your mate what you need, you'll gct it! It makes sense to me.

In the same workshop, another woman said, "He always forgets my birthday." My answer was another loud, *"Why don't you remind him before your birthday instead of being mean and having the "satisfaction" of blaming him later?"* Ouch! Send e-mails, leave notes on his pillow, whisper in his ear, "TUESDAY IS MY BIRTHDAY!" By the way, this applies to your anniversary as well. I think you will understand why I have little sympathy for men or women who are disappointed that their needs are not being met *if they haven't told their partner what they need!* It is not being fair to either your mate or yourself. Here's the plan:

- Pick up the mirror and ask yourself exactly what you need from your mate. Make a list. Then sit down with your mate and lovingly express your needs.

- Ask your mate what he/she needs from you. Take note and do your best to fullfil his/her needs.

Obviously, certain needs may be difficult for one or the other of you to fill. But since you understand your own needs and those of your mate, clarity will be there. And from a position of clarity, creative solutions can be found.

If your mate is not able to ask for what he/she needs, let me give you some clues. He/she would like to ask you the following:

Please take a deeper look.
Please know I have my own fears.
Please walk beside me.
Please let me know you love me.
Please let me know I bring you pleasure.
Please be caring and kind.

In the end, I guess we all need pretty much the same things.

8) *Stop the vicious circle that defensiveness creates.* Your mate criticizes you. Your normal way of reacting is defensively: "That is not true! And what about when you do ... (fill in the blanks)." And the cycle of anger and screaming begins. A dynamic has been set up in which your mate's negative behavior triggers negative behavior in yourself.

If you picked up the mirror, you would notice that your responses are about your need to be right. Ego! Ego! Ego! We have to move past our ego and change our negative reactions to his/her criticism. So when the next criticism comes your way, instead of responding defensively, you respond in a more constructive way. It sounds like this: "Hmm. You may be right. How would you suggest I handle it the next time?" An amazingly different response! A Higher Self, secure, loving and open kind of response. It doesn't mean that we have to go along with our mate's suggestion, but at least we have diffused the anger we are feeling. I would be surprised if you got a hostile answer with this approach. At the least it would be less hostile than you would get in the first instance.

This is a good example of blending energy instead of hitting each other over the head with ugly words. As we continue this Higher Self way of listening, we hear more and we learn more. Beautiful!

I understand that while loving words are easy to say under normal circumstances, when your buttons are pressed, they are very difficult to say. Even if you are feeling really angry, say the non-angry words anyway. You may be surprised to learn that your words will guide your emotions in a very effective way.

Defensiveness is just *a habit to be changed.* As we build our inner strength, we become less defensive and can "hear" in a softer way. Someone may criticize us, even verbally attack us, and we can say the ever-popular "thank you for sharing" without getting upset. And then, we can proceed to do what we feel is right for who we are.

Please keep in mind that criticism isn't always bad; in fact, it can be a valuable gift. We learn what we may be doing to alienate our partner or what we are doing to make our life more difficult. It's possible that our mate's criticism is actually valuable feedback, and we would be wise to listen.

9) ***Learn the beauty of silence.*** While in our relationship Mark had to learn to open up, I had to learn to be comfortable with silence—to be peacefully together with him without the need to connect with words. Eventually, I learned to connect with loving energy. I learned to communicate silently by relaxing and projecting the words "I love you" over and over again until I felt any inner tension melt and a feeling of love and connection gather in my heart. *Silent love.* Ultimately, I learned that silence can be beautiful. So try sending loving energy when silence is in the air. You will feel any tension quickly dissolving.

10) ***Validate your mate.*** We have to learn to look honestly at all the beautiful things our mate does. I'm suggesting a new kind of honesty called "appreciation." It makes our mate feel so good when we let him/her know the things we appreciate about him/her.

"I really appreciate you going to the bank for me."
"I really appreciate that you planned our next vacation."
"I really appreciate how you care for the kids."
"I really appreciate your warm and cuddly body."

This is so important for making our mate feel wonderful. And so important for making us notice all the beautiful things our mate does for us. This happily takes the focus off the negativity and, instead, fills our hearts with love.

11) ***Sometimes words are not necessary.*** There are those among us who have a difficult time saying, "I love you." But, as the saying goes, sometimes actions speak louder than words. Very often people we view as verbally unexpressive of their love or unaffectionate are constantly sending messages of love. For example:

I bring you a cup of coffee …	means …	I love you.
I earn a living for the both of us …	means …	I love you.
I take out the garbage …	means …	I love you.
I take care of the kids …	means …	I love you.
I am faithful to you …	means …	I love you.
I do the shopping …	means …	I love you.
I hold your hand …	means …	I love you.
I phone you during the day …	means …	I love you.

I'm sure that if we pay attention, we can fill pages with things that our mate does for us that can be translated as "I love you." When we understand this, we feel loved, and appreciate how blessed we are to have our mate in our lives.

For a variety of reasons, many men and women have a difficult time opening up in terms of their emotions. If this is true of your mate, who acts lovingly in so many ways, really take in the beautiful words of est founder Werner Erhard as he explains what he knows about the men or women who are having a difficult time communicating their love for us:

> "They have the capacity for love like yours and like mine which is absolute. The only thing bound up in their life is the expression of that capacity—so what you are getting is a bound expression of an absolute love for you and if you can accept that as their love for you and if you can be in ecstasy about that expression—if you can be joyful and celebrate that expression, your joy … your ecstasy … your being blown away by your relationship with them, I promise you will provide the heat necessary to melt whatever is there. Miracles will happen."[5]

Beautiful words to take into your heart.

12) *Learn openness in a safe place.* In a number of books, I have heralded the benefit of the group process. It provides a safe

space to open up and deal with what is hurting inside. Both men and women have benefited from groups over the years. Hearing that others experience the same problems is healing in itself. It makes us feel part of the whole. It rips down the walls of separation. We see that your story is my story, i.e., in some ways, everybody's story.

In the writing of *Opening Our Hearts to Men*, I had a desire to know the "man behind the mask" and was invited to attend a men's group. I listened as they talked. I was moved to tears. I loved every man there. Some were very angry; some were very loving. But they were all committed to learning more about life and love. What they said reveals a lot. I suggest you go to the source and read this very revealing chapter.[6]

In my own early days of learning and growing, I belonged to a number of groups. They were life-changing. I learned so much about myself and others. Later I conducted groups for both men and women. It is true that we live in a society where it is hard to be ourselves, but if we can be ourselves in the safety of the group, we can sometimes carry this openness with us into the real world.

So I urge all of you who are having difficulty communicating —men and women alike—to consider being part of a group, either a self-help group or a therapist-led group. And if you can't find one, start your own! I devote an entire chapter in *Dare to Connect* to finding or starting your own group.[7]

A word of warning: If you join a group, make sure it doesn't encourage a victim mentality. "Poor me, look what he/she did to me" has to be converted into "This is what happened. I want to learn from it and grow from it." It is important for all concerned to take responsibility for changing what doesn't work in their lives. Blame makes this impossible. The group needs to be about those in attendance becoming more loving and responsible people.

13) *Have patience.* Little by little, we have the power to transform the patterns that are now blocking communication with our loved one. It's important to have patience, mostly with ourselves,

as we learn how to look within to see where we are blocking communication and how we can improve it.

I know the above is a lot to take in. I suggest you really get the FEEL of healthy communication by reading through the above a number of times. Then start with the Love Lesson that feels right for you. Keep practicing until it feels easy and natural. Then move onto the next Love Lesson … and the next … and the next. One step at a time will always get you where you want to go. Don't give up. When you touch the heart of your mate with loving feelings and loving words, you will understand why it's definitely worth all the effort.

I love it all I love it all I love it all I love it all I love it all I love
it all I love it all I love it all I love it all I love it all I love it all
I love it all I love it all I love it all I love it all I love it all
I love it all I love it all I love it all I love it all I love it all I love
it all I love it all I love it all I love it all I love it all I love it all
I love it all I love it all I love it all love it all I love it all
I love it all I love it all I love it all I love it all I love it all I love
it all I love it all I love it all I love it all I love it all I love it all
I love it all I love it all I love it all I love it all I love it all
I love it all I love it all I love it all I love it all I love it all I love
it all I love it all I love it all I love it all I love it all I love it all
I love it all I love it all I love it all I love it all I love it all
I love it all I love it all I love it all I love it all I love it all I love
it all I love it all I love it all I love it all I love it all I love it all
I love it all I love it all I love it all I love it all I love it all
I love it all I love it all I love it all I love it all I love it all I love
it all I love it all I love it all I love it all I love it all I love it all
I love it all I love it all I love it all I love it all I love it all
I love it all I love it all I love it all I love it all I love it all I love
it all I love it all I love it all I love it all I love it all I love it all
I love it all I love it all I love it all I love it all I love it all I love
it all I love it all I love it all I love it all I love it all I love it all
I love it all I love it all I love it all I love it all I love it all
I love it all I love it all I love it all I love it all I love it all I love
it all I love it all I love it all I love it all I love it all I love it all
I love it all I love it all I love it all I love it all I love it all I love
it all I love it all I love it all I love it all I love it all I love it all
I love it all I love it all I love it all I love it all I love it all
I love it all I love it all I love it all I love it all I love it all I love
it all I love it all I love it all I love it all I love it all I love it all

Chapter 7

LOVING THE DIFFERENCES

To love someone is to see a miracle invisible to others.

—FRANCOIS MAURIAC

Don't you think it's a miracle that two people who are so different in so many ways can lovingly share a life together?

She snores; he forgets to take out the garbage; she leaves her makeup all over the countertop; he likes falling asleep with the television on; she likes going to bed early; he likes opera; she likes rock music … and on and on and on.

Why do some couples handle all these differences easily and effortlessly while others constantly fight? Well, I have a simple theory about how this works:

If you are filled with very loving feelings about your mate, your differences are easy to handle.

If you are filled with very unloving feelings about your mate, your differences are very hard to handle.

If my theory is correct, you would be wise to fill yourself with loving feelings toward your mate. Without these loving feelings, relatively unimportant differences can turn into serious incompatibilities.

To give you some filling-yourself-up-with-loving-feelings ideas, I created the following Love Chart and some suggestions for how to use it.

LOVE CHART

Unloving									Loving

1   2   3   4   5   6   7   8   9   10

critical   caring

blaming   grateful

disdainful   supportive

(and all that's negative)   (and all that's positive)

The Love Chart requires that you:

1) Take a really good look at how you normally relate to your mate, and then place yourself, truthfully, on the chart anywhere from 1 to 10.

Hmm. So where did you place yourself? If you have placed yourself at 10, congratulations! But remember, there's always more to learn, and even the best lovers among us can slip once in a while! If, like most of us, you've placed yourself on a number lower than 10, your goal is to move yourself step by step further on the side of love. You already have a very effective tool to help you do this: the mirror. The mirror reminds you to change what doesn't work. For example, it reminds you to:

104

- stop the blame,

- notice where you are not taking responsibility for your life,

- search your head and heart for ways to actively and openly be more loving toward your mate. (The Love Lessons are a great beginning.)

2) Once a week refer to the Love Chart to see if you have moved a little bit further on the side of love. If you have stopped blaming, taken responsibility for your life, and actively and openly behaved more lovingly toward your mate, you can't help but have moved yourself a little bit in the right direction. And as you keep practicing, your progress will continue. Don't worry if once in a while you slide backwards. Just pick yourself up and continue from where you left off. And your feeling of love will keep moving forward once again.

It could be that your mate is on the unloving side of the chart, that is, he/she treats you in a critical, blaming and disdainful way. Hopefully, as you move yourself further on the side of love, your new behavior will "rub off" on your mate. His/her attitude may dramatically change as yours does. If such is not the case, you might need to take another look at the relationship. (More about that in the Addendum.)

Always remember that your Higher Purpose is to become a more loving person. And, as you have already learned, your relationship is the greatest workshop going!

The key is to use every incompatibility in your relationship as a vehicle for learning how to be a more loving person.

Let me give you an example of how to handle a very common problem, "My husband's snoring is driving me crazy!" in a loving manner. This sounds like a trivial issue, but it's one that is a common cause of friction in a relationship. And it certainly needs to be dealt with, as it disturbs sleep. But *how it is dealt with is the important factor.* When love is high on the Love Chart, it is dealt with in a loving, caring way. When love is low on the Love Chart, it is dealt with in a critical and disdainful way.

Here are my suggestions for dealing with your mate's snoring in a loving, caring way:

No blame or annoyance allowed. First, remember that this is not your husband's fault and most likely you snore as well. I certainly do!

Discuss the problem lovingly. Explain in a non-blaming way that your sleep is being disrupted and this is affecting your health, energy and mood. Your sleep truly is important. Suggest to your partner that you work together to find a solution that works for both of you.

Get creative in finding a solution. Here are some ideas to get you started:

• Try earplugs. Remember, though, that some people are comfortable with them, but for others, they do not work.

• One man I know is seeking medical advice to handle the snoring. Consult your doctor as to what may or may not be available to help the snoring problem.

• Another man told me that when he gains weight, his snoring increases, so he tries to keep his weight down out of respect for his wife. Nice.

• Alarm clocks have become very innovative recently. For example, you can buy alarm clocks with a variety of sounds, such as the ocean, birds singing or even just "white noise." Pick a sound you like. It is the white noise that does it for one woman I talked to. It masks the snoring in a way that makes it acceptable. She actually finds the white noise quite soothing.

• Get it out of your head that sleeping in separate rooms is necessarily indicative of a failure in the relationship. If snoring (or other sleep issues) is a problem, sleeping in separate rooms (if you have an extra room available) can help the relationship considerably. Cuddling in the morning and cuddling before you go to sleep helps keep you high on the side of love and caring. Ironically, many couples I spoke to do sleep in separate rooms but are embarrassed to admit it. How silly is that! Don't lay a trip on yourself if, for one reason or the other, you choose to sleep in separate rooms. It can be a loving arrangement.

• One couple I interviewed told me the following: "It sounds corny but it's true: When one of us is snoring—and at times we both do—we simply note to ourselves how happy we are to be together. In this way, we have made our mate's snoring a "comfort factor" in our lives. In fact, when we are apart, we joke that we miss each other's snoring! The good news is that neither one of us snores loudly enough for it to cause a sleep problem for the other, and often a gentle pulling on the blankets stops the snoring in its tracks. If the snoring were louder on the part of either of us, we would have to come up with another solution. And we would!" Yes, they were able to make snoring a comfort factor in their relationship. I love this!

These are just a few ideas relative to snoring. You can see that when the love and caring is high, snoring is just something to handle: it isn't a detriment to the love in the relationship. When the love and caring is low, blame and disdain are activated and no creative solutions are forthcoming.

You often need creativity, in addition to love, to solve problems in a relationship. Think. Get out of the box. I will wager that if you look hard enough, you can come up with a loving solution to almost anything.

Another common complaint, as I mentioned earlier, is the "up-ness" or "down-ness" of the toilet seat. It is comical how the toilet seat becomes the focus of so much upset in a relationship, isn't it? She wants it down; he leaves it up. Of course, there really isn't any right or wrong in this matter. I mean, I have never seen any toilet seat instructions that say that the seat must be up … or down. Have you? One can adjust one's mindset to either.

Maybe the toilet seat issue isn't really about the toilet seat! Maybe it's about where we score on the Love Chart. If he scores high on the Love Chart, the man probably will remember to put the seat down because he wants to please his mate. On the other hand, if she scores high on the Love Chart, the woman probably will be totally okay with the seat being up. Or she may lovingly say:

"Sweetheart, I would appreciate it so much if you trained yourself to put the toilet seat down. It looks gross to me to have the seat up. I don't know why, but that's how I feel. I would really appreciate your doing this for me."

This is a lot more likely to evoke a satisfactory response than:

"You are so disgusting and inconsiderate—always leaving the toilet seat up."

Not very loving! Again, is it really disgusting and inconsiderate to leave the toilet seat up? Some of us don't really care one way or the other. This isn't a right or wrong situation, but there is no question that if both parties are low on the Love Chart, the toilet seat becomes something else to separate them.

The need to control the toilet seat is also an addictive demand of the kind I talked about in Chapter 5, or something we need to control in order to be happy. If there is anything we need to move to the level of a preference instead of a demand, it truly is the toilet seat! And when we move ourselves on the side of love, the position of the toilet seat definitely loses its significance.

And how about when one of you is always late? Grrr. I see many couples arguing about this issue. Here are some suggestions:

- If you are consistently late, you may have an erroneous sense of time. Here's the rule: leave TWICE as much time as you think it will take to get to your destination. This is often what people who are sensitive about time do. (Thankfully Mark and I are on the same wavelength about this one!)

- If you still can't manage to be on time, pick up the mirror and ask yourself why. Could it be that you are on the unloving side of the Love Chart? Resentment can often make us late without our consciously being aware of it. In any case, understand that *being late is disrespectful of another's time.* Not nice! It's time to get conscious about time and not keep your mate or anyone else waiting.

- If it is your mate who is always late, follow the guidelines in the snoring example above: No blame, talk about it lovingly and come up with a creative solution together on the side of love. Alternatively, you can make your desire for your partner to be on time a *preference,* not an *addiction* that causes anger and upset. While Mark is always on time (actually early), a few of my friends are not. To keep myself on the side of love, I have taught myself to enjoy alone time in restaurants waiting for my tardy friends. I people-watch (one of my favorite activities) and I relax. I don't make myself miserable—which makes my time with my friends much more enjoyable when they finally do arrive! You can do the same thing as you wait for your mate. Peace restored.

How about when one of you is messy and the other is neat? The questions become:

If he/she is messy: "How can I react in a more loving way?"

If you are the messy one: "What can I do to be more considerate of my partner's feelings?"

I score high on the side of messiness, but because I also score high on the side of love, I work very hard to pick up after myself. And I must say I am relatively successful. How do I know? Mark was away on business for a few days and I reverted back to my natural self. Within a very short time, the house truly was a mess! By the time, Mark came home, however, I had put it all back together again as I looked forward to his return. I realize it's all choice. And my choice is not to inflict my messiness on him. I love the words of author and spiritual teacher Marianne Williamson:

"I carry all the power of goodness and I am going to act from that power. I could act from love or I could be a total slob. It's up to me."[1]

Oh, that's so true—literally and figuratively!

If your mate is the slob, just understand that neatness isn't one of his/her priorities. When you're high on the Love Chart, it is easy to make his/her neatness a preference rather than an addiction. Find a way to deal with it lovingly. It helps to:

Focus the bulk of your attention on the good things your mate brings into your life.

In this way, you won't let his/her sloppiness pull you away from love.

And how do you handle the disagreements that always pop up in any relationship? Do you keep to the point or do you stray into dangerous territory? Here's an example:

"I feel bad that you didn't consult me about the plans you made for the weekend. In the future let's talk about it together before either one of us makes any plans for the weekend. That would make me happy."

That's clear, understandable, and can lead to constructive discussion. If, however, you wander off point, it can sound like this:

"I feel bad you didn't consult me about the plans you made for the weekend. You always do this to me. You are so inconsiderate. I don't know why I stay with you."

Ouch! Not good. Very unloving and painful to our mate. If we are not on the side of love, it is very easy to become psychologically numb to the pain we cause our mate. We are so selfishly caught up

111

in our own feelings that we can't see that our mate has feelings as well. Again, it's a choice. Do you want to become a more loving person or not? If you do, then *keep to the point* when something upsets you and handle it in a loving way.

The above are just a few of the minor differences that can cause upset between two people. I'm sure we all can think of many, many more. Again, while we can't control our mate, *we can control our own reactions to our differences.* Just use it all as a way to practice becoming a more loving person. It is also important to remember to keep focusing on the beauty that your mate brings into your life. The light that shines within us shines much brighter as we focus on the good rather than the bad.

You now have your marching orders. Your goal is to:

INCREASE THE LOVE AND DECREASE THE UPSET.

Yes, it can be a challenge, but the rewards can be great. When we pick up the mirror instead of the magnifying glass, we are moving ourselves from the Lower Self to the Higher Self, where love lives.

As we become Higher Self thinkers, we are very conscious about our effect on our partner. We constantly ask ourselves, "Do I make him/her feel good or do I cause distress?" If our answer is the latter, we ask ourselves, "What can I do to change this pattern?" We then find our way back to the side of love once again. Make no mistake about it, it's a very beautiful journey.

As you learn to become a more loving person, your mate may not follow your example. In no way am I advocating that you allow yourself to be walked all over. One of my favorite expressions is, "There's nothing as unattractive as footprints on the face." How true. There are times when it is very wise to walk away. Just understand that someone's bad behavior (including our own) is a symptom of the fear and pain they hold inside. This understanding helps us to stay—or leave—with love in our heart.

LOVE LESSONS

1) *Choose your mate's joy.* There is a silent dialogue that goes on within the heads of loving people when they are thinking in a caring way. It goes like this:

> **I want this.**
> **You want that.**
> **I want your happiness.**
> **Therefore let's do it your way.**

Loving indeed! Let me give you an example from my own life. There is a lovely little restaurant Mark and I often go to for lunch. It has both indoor and outdoor seating. I usually prefer to sit indoors, as it is often very sunny outside and there are no places to sit in the shade. I assumed Mark also enjoyed sitting inside, as he always headed toward our favorite inside table. Therefore I was surprised to learn that when he goes to the restaurant with friends or for a business meeting, he usually sits outside. I said, "But you don't like sitting outside." He said, "I prefer eating outside, but I know that you enjoy eating inside. And it makes me happy to make you happy." Wow! You may think this is a little thing, but actually, in terms of the Love Chart, it's way up there! Yes, Mark has taught me much about love.

There are many ways in which we can choose our partner's joy: watching a television show he/she wants to watch, giving him/her the last piece of dessert … you get the point. There is no question that even very minor things are important in helping to create a beautiful love.

2) *Be your partner's best friend.* When a relationship is on the downslide, one thing you will notice is how much better we treat our friends than our partner. We say things to our partner that we would rarely, if ever, say to our friends. Anger and resentment can get very ugly indeed.

It is important to become conscious of our effect on our partner. Instead of building up our mate's confidence, we too often are into criticism. When we criticize our mate, we are definitely cutting off our nose to spite our face. Let me ask you: Why would he/she want to be around you if you are constantly being critical? *Would you want to be around you?* Hence, you know your task … *to train yourself to be the person you would like to be around*: your best friend. And that requires you to stay conscious.

Probably the most important question you can ask yourself throughout your relationship is, "If he/she were my best friend, how would I be acting?" In *Feel the Fear and Do It Anyway,* I taught you how to play the game of *act-as-if.* When it comes to love, it goes like this:

"If I were his/her best friend, what would I say?"
Then say it."

"If I were his/her best friend, what would I do?"
Then do it."

Even if you don't feel like saying it or doing it, act-as-if you really do want to say it and do it; that is, *tell a lie on the side of love.* Little by little you will *live into the feeling* of what it is to really be a best friend to your partner. How a person handles conflicts or anything else in the relationship depends on the strength of their friendship. And your ultimate goal is to become your partner's best friend.

3) *Let go of your models of right and wrong.* Yes, every day we come face to face with the differences between our mate and ourselves. But when we let go of our need for control, we can just let things be the way they are and not get hung up over our pictures of perfection. I love the following words of Ken Keyes:

"As we reach behind the models in our mind, we can see the way each individual is beautiful, capable and loveable. By learning to accept people as they are, we can see the preciousness of each person. By working on our addictive models of how the world should be, we begin to radiate an ever-widening acceptance and love."[2]

Beautiful. We have to stop judging our mate and, instead, work on our reactions, i.e., our need for our mate to be a certain way.

By the way, when we pick up the mirror, we realize that we are not perfect either. In *Opening Our Hearts to Men,* I describe a women's workshop I conducted. At one point I asked the women to yell out what is wrong with men. They came up with a LONG list. I then asked them to yell out what is wrong with women. Being honest with themselves, they once again came up with a LONG list. I then told them, when we have fixed all that is wrong with ourselves, we can then work on the men. In the midst of their laughter, they got the point!

I mustn't forget to mention that I then asked them to yell out what's wonderful about men and what's wonderful about women. As they did so, the whole energy in the room changed into light-ness and love—just as it does in life when we appreciate the beauty of who we are and who our mates are. Fantastic!

it's all happening perfectly it's all happening perfectly
it's all happening perfectly it's all happening perfectly
it's all happening perfectly it's all happening perfectly
it's all happening perfectly it's all happening perfectly
it's all happening perfectly it's all happening perfectly
it's all happening perfectly it's all happening perfectly
it's all happening perfectly it's all happening perfectly
it's all happening perfectly it's all happening perfectyl
it's all happening perfectly it's all happening perfectly
it's all happening perfectly it's all happening perfectly
it's all happening perfectly it's all happening perfectly
it's all happening perfectly it's all happening perfectly
it's all happening perfectly it's all happening perfectly
it's all happening perfectly it's all happening perfectly
it's all happening perfectly it's all happening perfectly
it's all happening perfectly it's all happening perfectly
it's all happening perfectly it's all happening perfectly
it's all happening perfectly it's all happening perfectly
it's all happening perfectly it's all happening perfectly
it's all happening perfectly it's all happening perfectly
it's all happening perfectly it's all happening perfectly
it's all happening perfectly it's all happening perfectly
it's all happening perfectly it's all happening perfectly
it's all happening perfectly it's all happening perfectly
it's all happening perfectly it's all happening perfectly
it's all happening perfectly it's all happening perfectly
it's all happening perfectly it's all happening perfectly
it's all happening perfectly it's all happening perfectly
it's all happening perfectly it's all happening perfectly
it's all happening perfectly it's all happening perfectly
it's all happening perfectly it's all happening perfectly
it's all happening perfectly it's all happening perfectly
it's all happening perfectly it's all happening perfectly

Chapter 8

WHEN LIFE INTERFERES WITH LOVE

A relationship is a gold mine. We would be much
richer if we mined the gold.

—SUSAN JEFFERS

Yes, a relationship is a gold mine. It has the potential for teaching us so many things about giving, loving and caring. This
is because life hands us so many difficult situations that can interfere with love, and we need to learn how to handle them. They
include problems with money, children, in-laws, aging, retire-
ment, overwork, religion and on and on and on. When problems
occur, that's our signal to mine the gold, and that means learning
how to become a more loving person in the middle of it all.

I was very moved by a recent television segment depicting the
difficulties encountered—and handled—by a Sikh woman and a
Jewish man who had been married for twenty-five years. Many,
many problems came up as a result of the differences in their reli-
gions, especially after their children were born. Their families,
their societies and the world in general were against their marriage

and fought them in many profoundly disturbing ways. The couple said *it was their determination to keep their love a priority* that kept their love alive. They learned and grew from it all. They "mined the gold" and today their love is very strong and very rich indeed.

In all things we need to determine to *keep our love a priority* if we expect to create a lasting love. Sometimes this is easier said than done. We all have our own issues. But whatever these issues are, the basic rules of love apply. And it is these rules that we all need to learn in order to help us strengthen our sense of self—and our love. Let me describe three common and potentially damaging situations and how the basic rules of love apply. Even if these three issues are not a factor in your life, read them anyway. You can apply many, if not all, of the principles to what is happening in your own relationship ... and in your own life. (Note that because of the format of this chapter, the Love Lessons are included within, instead of at the end.)

INTERFERING IN-LAWS*

First, let me say that many in-laws are wonderful people who contribute to, enjoy and love their family the very best they can. But there certainly are those who give us much opportunity for learning and growing!

Janet has managed to keep her love a priority in the face of her *very* difficult mother-in-law, Sophia. On my visits to Janet's home, I've personally seen Sophia's judgmental and unappreciative behavior, and I must admit that I have to restrain myself from saying something very mean. But Janet is amazingly impervious to her mother-in-law's behavior. She just doesn't let it get to her—at least most of the time!

I asked her how she does it. She said, "I want Sophia to be a part of our lives for the sake of my husband and my children."

---

*Of course, this can be adapted to your own parents. It also applies to the parents of couples who are not married.

(Note the caring.) Janet also is sympathetic toward her mother-in-law, who has had a very difficult life. (Note the compassion.) She said, "I just don't let her affect me in a negative way. I've created this imaginary protective ray around me, and her negativity just doesn't get through." (Note the creativity.) She has explained to her two sons that their grandmother is an unhappy person, and they should pay attention only to the nice things she does for them. (Note how she focuses on the good.) Janet is a shining example of how to stay in the Higher Self when one of our in-laws is stuck in the Lower Self.

This isn't to say that Janet doesn't have her limits. For example, Sophia joined her family on a trip to France a few years ago. Sophia was so difficult that Janet decided that her mother-in-law will not travel with them again. And she has stuck to her guns. When Sophia complained that she wasn't invited on the next vacation, Janet simply replied, "I love you but we don't travel well together." And while her mother-in-law tried to argue, Janet kept calmly repeating her "mantra": "I love you but we don't travel well together." End of story. (Note the healthy boundary she has created.)

Janet is a model of caring, compassion, creativity and appreciation while maintaining a healthy boundary with her mother-in-law. If you incorporate all of this in your relationship with your in-laws (and parents and family), you definitely will be a lot happier—and so will your mate.

Here are some further suggestions as to what you can do to protect your relationship if one or both of your in-laws are getting in the way:

- Don't argue with your mate about your in-laws or put him/her in the middle. He/she has a multitude of feelings related to his/her parents having to do with loyalty, guilt, love and other parent/child feelings. Don't make him/her have to choose. This is not a caring thing to do. Lovingly act on your own to heal the situation as best as you can.

- Support your mate if his/her parents try to make him/her feel badly. For example, if they complain that your mate doesn't do enough for them, remind them of the loving things he/she does do.

- Keep in mind that while some in-laws are very appreciative of our efforts on their behalf, some are "unfillable." You can give and give and give and they won't be satisfied. This is just who they are and it is doubtful you will change them. Keep your love high and let their criticisms go by the wayside.

- Stop being defensive. Alice, one of my students, remembered her mother-in-law commenting that Alice's cupboards were a mess. Instead of being angry, she said, "I agree. Why don't you clean them? It would be a great help to me." So her mother-in-law cleaned her cupboards, happy to be of use. A beautiful example of blending energies! By not being defensive, Alice was able to make it a win-win situation.

- Many problems arise with in-laws when you have children. Grandparents often love to tell you how to raise your kids. Again, put aside your defensiveness. Listen and possibly learn. Some in-laws really can teach you a lot. They've lived a lot longer than you have and can probably pass on valuable information. In addition, they may make great babysitters!

- If your in-law's advice is intrusive and critical, take a loving stand. Don't act like a child yourself by whining, pouting, getting angry and the like. Be very clear that you are the parents of your children and you are in charge. When I say, "Be very clear," I mean firmly, but gently, tell them that this is one area where you and your mate rule. "I love you and I rule." Your in-laws really may be wonderful people but we have to create boundaries when it comes to how we want to raise our children.

- Thank them for any good they do. Whatever your situation, you usually can find some good. And if you can't find any good, at least thank them for creating your terrific mate!

- Be interested in their lives. Really get to know them. I suspect their lives have been filled with many experiences that will surprise you. Some will have overcome great difficulties and worked hard throughout their lives in order to provide for their children. Delving deeper into their lives will make you feel closer to them.

- If your in-laws don't live nearby, keep them involved with your family through photos, e-mails, phone calls, etc. They will be very appreciative.

- If they live very close, lovingly protect your boundaries as you honor their boundaries. If they don't honor your boundaries, you might consider moving further away. Creating more distance often can create a better relationship!

- Stop your mind from going over and over things that may have upset you in the past. They truly did—and still do—the best they can, given who they are as human beings. Replace negative thoughts about the past with positive thoughts about how you are going to change your actions and reactions in the present and the future.

- Send loving light. Simply close your eyes and send them loving light, wishing them all wonderful things. Do it often. As you have already learned, your positive loving energy is contagious—even when it involves your in-laws.

- Tell them you love them. If you say it often enough, you actually can live into the feeling of love.

- Lighten up! Don't take it all that seriously. Learn from Janet, who takes all of it—well, most of it—in her stride and lets very little interfere with her appreciation of her many blessings.

Once again, as is the theme throughout this book, just keep remembering that it isn't about what your in-laws are doing; it is about your REACTION to what they are doing. As you can see, in-laws—good or bad—make perfect "practice people." As we keep our eye focused on our Higher Purpose, that of becoming a more loving person, our in-laws definitely can give us great practice. They help us to push through our own issues relating to competition, control, our need to be right, our need for approval ... and much more.

Remember that any "bad" behavior on their part comes from their own insecurities, as does yours. You be the one to grow up and act in a loving manner. You be the one to take what is, work with it, learn from it and make something positive out of it. Again, it is doubtful you will ever change your in-laws. Hopefully, your loving actions will rub off on them. In any case, when you do the above, *you'll* be a much happier person—and so will your mate!

CHILDREN

Yes, in-laws can cause problems in a relationship, but nowhere near the amount of problems that children—cute as they are—can bring! I agree totally with writer and director Nora Ephron, who said: "A baby is a hand grenade tossed into a marriage."[1] And if we truly want to keep our love alive, our goal has to be to catch that grenade before it explodes and wrecks what was once a beautiful love. One young father told me with great sadness in his voice:

> My wife and I were so in love. We looked forward to the birth of our child with great anticipation. We decorated the nursery and enjoyed preparing for it all. When our son finally arrived, we were ecstatic. But not for long. What we weren't prepared for was the reality of caring for a child. We weren't prepared for the exhaustion, the resentment that started to build between the two of us, and the lack of freedom, which prior to the baby we had taken for granted. This didn't mean we didn't love our son, but it did mean that ultimately we stopped loving each other. And by the time our son was four we were no longer able to live together.

This story points out one of the reasons that parents have so many big problems when they have a child: They are totally unprepared to deal with the realities of children—the constant attention that helpless children require; the fatigue; the intrusion in their togetherness; the decrease in sexual activity … and so much more. In *I'm Okay … You're a Brat,* I explain in great detail the difficulties children bring to relationships. I suggest you read this book whether you have children or are considering having them. It will remove a lot of your upset and take a lot of guilt off your shoulders. A "conspiracy of silence" keeps most of us in the dark about how a child changes our lives and what to do about it.

Of course, many couples thrive when children are born. They have those "loving being a parent" genes, as I call them. They thoroughly love having children in the house … and can't wait to have more. But the rest of us are shocked as we watch our relationship being torn apart by the introduction of a child into the household. We wonder, "What happened?" (I see many of your heads nodding out there.)

There is no question that children can be all-consuming. And as we are caring for our little ones, we forget to care about our relationship. Let me give you a few suggestions for handling the inevitable conflicts in a relationship when children arrive.

1. *Handle the resentment.* I speak from experience on this one. Let me reveal something I wrote in my journal so many years ago as it relates to my own inappropriate feelings getting in the way of love:

> "My life took on the feeling of a monotonous routine, made even more difficult with the baby's bouts of colic. They seemed to occur every night between eleven and three in the morning. One long night, as I paced the floor of the nursery trying to calm my screaming baby, uncontrollable tears started to flow down my face. I was slowly hit with the realization that the fun and games were ended and we weren't playing house any more. The reality hit me with a stunning blow.
>
> The tears kept streaming down my face as I continued to walk in circles with my little one. As I tried to ease his pain, I realized that there was no longer anyone to ease mine. My husband had his responsibilities and I had mine. I deeply resented him as he slept in the other room. I so wanted him to take over, yet I couldn't expect him to be up all night and go to work the next day. And for the first time, I started to see myself as a "victim." I was the one stuck at home—taken out of the mainstream of

life. Strangely, I held little resentment for my son. We were in it together. We were both helpless and pathetic. It was "poor us" alone in this world. My husband became the enemy."

Totally irrational thinking on my part, I know. Had I known then what I know today, I would have grown up and noticed that while I had little control over my screaming child or my sleeping husband, *I did have control over my reaction to what was happening.* I would have told myself:

"Yes, I'm upset. I'm exhausted. But I know this too shall pass. I need to focus on this beautiful little life I have in my hands and do everything I can to help him grow up into a healthy, happy and responsible adult. I have to focus on the fact that I have a very giving husband who is supporting us financially. I have to be creative in figuring out a way that I can enjoy my child and still be in this world."

Yes, I ultimately learned how to "enjoy my child and still be in this world." But my initial resentment took a lot out of my first marriage. No question about it. And I learned that resentment is a totally powerless feeling, a sign that we are not taking responsibility for our lives. From the above, you can tell I had a great deal to learn about living with a sense of power and love.

Of course, men too have their resentments when it comes to children. While some love the entrance of a child into their lives, some resent having increased financial responsibility. Some also resent the fact that they can't spend more time with their children because they have to work so hard. Some resent their partner's attention going to the child instead of to them. Some resent the diminished sex that often accompanies the birth of a child. Yes, sex often goes out the window once a child is born. (Learn more about this in Chapter 10.)

You can see that both men and women have to grow up and work through any resentment of each other so they can be very creative in finding solutions to the issues tearing the relationship apart. My suggestion is that every time you begin feeling resentful toward your mate, you just pick up the mirror and say to yourself:

> This is not my mate's fault. It is time for me to take responsibility for the fact that I now have a young being in my care. I have to grow up and do what-ever it takes to create a meaningful and loving life for myself and my mate while caring responsibly for the needs of my child.

This kind of attitude brings forward your strength and creativity … and resentment disappears. So remember: Put your blame in the right place. Your mate didn't create the difficulties. And it certainly isn't your child's fault. By placing the upset in the right place—the reality of parenthood—you are able to see your mate in a more compassionate way.

When the resentment disappears, you are able to hold hands once again and work as a team to solve the problems that children bring with them. Hopefully the anger and resentment, which block the flow of love, will be replaced by a sense of the two of you doing something meaningful together.

2. ***Don't let equality go down the drain.*** While men and women often experience a sense of equality when they are child-free, most of us haven't yet perfected the concept of equality after a child is born. Traditional roles frequently

sneak in to make women the primary caretakers of the children. For some, this works beautifully; for others, it is a catastrophe!

It is so important that you and your partner sit down together to determine what works better for both of you. Otherwise, resentment will clearly be on the horizon instead of the beauty that can come from jointly raising a child. This is one area of a relationship that needs the utmost creativity so that women who want a career don't lose their place in the workplace and men don't miss out on being with and caring for their child.

By the way, don't believe the popular myth that only women can be the nurturers when it comes to children. Some women are great nurturers; some aren't. Some men are great nurturers; some aren't. In fact, more and more men are choosing to be the stay-at-home parent as their wives go out to work. So many men display nurturing skills that are beautiful to behold.

Relevant to this point: A recent story in the press reported that a number of very successful women are quitting their jobs to work part-time so they can spend more time with their children. Perhaps one day you will read a story in the press that reports that a number of very successful women *and men* are quitting their jobs to work part-time so they can spend more time with their children.

3. *Create alone time ... together.* For obvious reasons, when you have a child many of the intimate moments are gone. A third person has entered the picture—in more ways than one. As I describe in *I'm Okay ... You're a Brat,* if you look around you see:

Mothers catering to the needs of their children
—*no father in sight.*

127

Fathers catering to the needs of their children
—*no mother in sight.*

Parents catering to the needs of their children
—*no "togetherness" in sight.*

This is in contrast to:

Couples walking together arm and arm, hand in hand,
kissing, talking, hugging, watching the world together
—*no children in sight.*[2]

You don't have to believe me; just become a people
watcher as I am. When it relates to togetherness with your
mate, children—through no fault of their own— are true
separators.

It is important to do all you can to find time to be
together with your partner ... alone. Unfortunately, in
recent times, parents have been made to feel guilty if they
don't spend more and more time with their children. By
definition, this dictates that parents spend less and less
time alone with each other. While in the not-too-distant
past, parents often went out in the evenings or on vacation
to renew their closeness and passion for each other, now
too often the children are accompanying them. I know
couples who have not left their children with a baby-sitter
for years! Where's the privacy? Where's the romance?
Remember that *nourishing your relationship is as important as nourishing your children.* Children ultimately leave
home; your goal is to keep your mate (or yourself) from
leaving home!

Yes, children must be cared for responsibly and lovingly,
but there are many ways to take care of a child responsibly
and lovingly without destroying your relationship with your

partner. Despite what many "guilt-gurus" may tell you, I believe it is much healthier for children to experience a variety of care-takers. It broadens their experience and allows them to feel secure in the realization that there are many people out there who can care for them in a loving way.*

Responsible child-minders, willing grandparents and friends are all around you. One woman created a babysitting group to take turns caring for each other's children. One woman with older children told me she often arranges a romantic rendezvous with her husband in the middle of the afternoon while her children are at school. Think creatively in order to nourish the togetherness of your relationship.

4. ***Handle your fatigue.*** Both you and your mate need proper rest. It goes without saying that the fatigue that occurs from taking care of very young children can only create difficulty in your relationship. Find ways of getting help. Again, you don't have to do it alone. Nor should you. Hillary Clinton was very wise when she reminded us that "it takes a village" to raise a child.[3] We do better—and our children do better—when we draw from the many sources of nourishment and experience that are out there for us—and our children.

5. ***Don't fight over how to raise a child.*** Maybe you're right; maybe you're wrong. What I have to say may surprise you. Every child is different: therefore one method doesn't work for all. In addition, there are many factors outside the family that affect how a child grows up. I call these factors the child's "Circle of Being." A child's Circle of Being includes their genes, their friends, their society,

---

*I encourage you to read *I'm Okay ... You're a Brat* in which I explain the research. There is evidence that children do just as well, if not better in certain areas, with multiple care-takers.

their teachers and on and on and on.[4] Once again, the experts don't know it all. As far as I am concerned, any expert that says he or she KNOWS how to raise a healthy child is very ill-informed and needs to go back to school. I have seen children given the worst kind of treatment during their young life and they grow up great; and I have seen children given the best kind of treatment during their young life and they grow up horribly. It's all chancy!

So when your mate does things that you think are not healthy for the child, for example, if one of you is lenient and the other is strict, just remember that maybe you're right, maybe you're wrong. And because nobody knows for sure, *differing parenting styles should not create conflict*. Just do your best. Allow your mate to do his/her best. Keep remembering, nobody knows for sure.

6. ***Don't feel guilty if you are having difficulty with your child and/or your mate.*** Because of the conspiracy of silence, you often don't hear parents talking about their problems once children come into the picture. They just pretend that all is well. Trust me when I tell you that for many parents, all is not well! My interviews with many parents for *I'm Okay ... You're a Brat* proved this. While many started out talking about how grand parenthood is, many became upset and even cried as I dug a little deeper.

If parenthood is difficult for you, I suggest you be one of the first to tell your truth; it may help others open up to the difficulties they are facing. As the difficulties are exposed, the guilt disappears and solutions appear. Also learn as much as you can from those who seem to have done it all quite successfully. Ask them how they got through the raising of their child with love in their hearts not only for their children but for their partner as well. As you focus on finding healing solutions you will find them. Trust me.

MONEY

Money is another potential source of huge problems in relationships. Most of us worry about it; many of us fight about it; some relationships end because of it. Once again, fear is at the heart of most problems with money. Fear creates insecurity, disappointment, resentment and anger. Some speculate that money is the biggest cause of divorce. Maybe it is; maybe it isn't. In any case, it is very clear that money issues can be very difficult to deal with.

Tied up with money are issues such as self-respect, control, survival and inappropriate expectations. All have to do with a deep insecurity. Our societal training is somewhat responsible for this. Men have been socialized to be the providers and women have been socialized to be taken care of by a man. Even today, after women have made so many advances in the world of work, old expectations linger. We have to remain very aware when these old expectations get in the way of love.

Ideally, we work together with our mate when it comes to money. This is one of those areas where agreement as to a financial strategy really helps. But there is much we can do on our own as well. Let me give you a few suggestions to help you deal with your upsets about money:

1. *Take responsibility.* How do you take responsibility on your own? It looks like this:

> • Learn as much as you can about money in general as well as your financial situation as a couple so you won't be blindsided if problems occur.

> • If you spend too much, (and, honestly, you know if you do), stop it. It isn't fair either to you or your mate. I actually know a woman who spent an outrageous amount of money and, when financial problems occurred, blamed her husband for not

stopping her from spending so much! Yes, it would have been wise for her husband to have stepped in and stopped her, but his claim was that he loved her and wanted her to be happy. The solution? Each partner needs to take responsibility for their own part in their financial mess and then work together to clean the mess up.

• If your mate is the spender and you are concerned about saving money, you must discuss this with him/her. I know couples who have racked up huge credit card debt when one of the partners couldn't control his/her spending. Unfortunately, both of you are responsible for the payment. If your mate refuses to take your well-being into consideration, it is time to think about getting out of a situation that is not serving you.

• Always be prepared to take care of yourself financially. Stay-at-home parents need to keep up with their skills so that, if need be, they can step into a money-earning role. Don't put all the pressure on your mate. We need to support one another. The knowledge that either one of us can take care of ourselves financially is a big bonus in a relationship.

Hopefully, as you begin taking responsibility for understanding what is going on with your money and acting in a responsible way, your mate will take responsibility as well. Dealing with money needs to be a joint venture. I know many men/women who allow their mate to handle all the money issues and don't have a clue as to what their financial situation is. This is not wise and can at some point lead to great difficulty in the relationship.

Men tend to feel bad if they are not providing enough money for the family, even in these days when so many women work. They feel a sense of powerlessness when they lose a job, or do not readily find one when needs come up and the money isn't there. It hurts. At the same time, some women (and thankfully this is changing) see their men as inadequate if they are not bringing in enough money. This combination can make the lack of money a relationship-killer.

In today's world, this kind of thinking is truly out of date. We need to revise our thinking by picking up the mirror and asking, "Why am I letting my conditioning about money keep me stuck in the past?" Relax and let yourself feel the peace in knowing that you BOTH are responsible for being able to take care of yourselves financially.

Here is a perfect example of the peace of mind this understanding can bring: A young man went into a new business venture with great trepidation. He spent a lot of joint savings (with his wife's participation in the decision), which left him very nervous about having enough money. He says he would have just given up if it weren't for the encouragement of his wife. Although she admitted having her own fears about money, her ability to cheer him on rested in her confidence that she could earn enough money to carry them over. What a relief!

It is key for all of us to know that we are capable of taking care of ourselves financially. If you are a woman or man who has decided to stay home and take care of the children, keep your skills honed. If your partner loses his/her job, you then are secure in the knowledge that you can contribute to the cause. Taking care of children plays havoc with money and careers. If you are a person who worries about money, staying at home is not a good idea. You need to take responsibility and not put the all the burden of your worries on your mate. Here are some further suggestions:

- **If your partner gets a fabulous new job:** Be positive and make sure your own insecurity does not keeping him/her from growing. (Yes, there are those who get very insecure when their partner is growing.) Remember to work on your own self-esteem so that you can enjoy your mate's—and your own—good fortune.

- **If your partner loses his/her job:** Make sure that you handle your own insecurities about money so that you do not hurt your partner, who is hurting already. Always be prepared to take up the slack.

- **If one or both of you spends too much money:** Being in debt creates huge problems in a relationship. Get professional help if either one of you can't stop spending. Consult financial experts and make an effective plan for moving your financial security in the right direction.

- **If one of you gets a good job in another part of the country:** Moving can create much upset and confusion in a family. Be determined that you will find something wonderful in your new home. If you don't embrace the excitement and joy a new move can bring, you run the risk of missing an important opportunity for learning more about life. You also run the risk of hurting your relationship.

- **If one or both of you works long hours:** Ideally partners need to make it a priority to spend as much time together as they can, but sometimes the work of one or both demands a lot of time ... especially in recent years. If this is true for you, find ways of constantly connecting, through phone calls, e-mails, text messages, long hugs and kisses at the end of the day, meaningful vacations where possible, and the like. Get creative in making real or virtual time together.

Yes, money can be a difficult issue in your relationship—or it can be an opportunity to bring you and your partner closer together. Again, learn as much as you can about becoming a more loving person. In this way, the "problem" of money becomes a wonderful opportunity.

Above I've mentioned just a few of the life experiences that can get in the way of love. I'm sure you can think of many more. But whatever situation we are faced with, we will be well-served by keeping the following essentials in mind:

- It's all an opportunity to learn and grow.

- Don't blame your mate. Take responsibility for your reactions to it all.

- Get very creative in learning how to honor yourself while honoring your mate.

- Whatever is interfering with your love, seek guidance through books, counselors, workshops or whatever. Just learn as much as you can.

- Take ACTION to change what isn't working.

- Keep working on your self-esteem. High self-esteem allows us to love and honor our mate while loving and honoring ourselves.

- Remember your Higher Purpose mantra:

    It's all happening perfectly. Whatever happens in my life, I'll handle it. I'll learn from it. I'll grow from it. I'll make it a triumph!

Here's your goal: Recognize a potential problem, work with it, grow from it. In all things, look in your trusty mirror and ask yourself, "Am I letting my needs control this relationship, or am I letting my heart control this relationship?" Only you know the answer to that question. If you determine that you are blaming and not taking responsibility, your needs are definitely getting in the way. If you support your mate and at the same time feel your own sense of power and love, your heart is controlling the relationship.

We can't let life get in the way of love. We must commit to making our relationship a priority. The need to feel loved is very important in a marriage, but it is my belief that, in order to have a good marriage, the ability to love is just as important. No relationship is smooth all the time; they all go through patches of change and adjustment. But if we keep picking up the mirror we can always find a way of being at peace and being more compassionate to the person we love. In this way, our love grows and grows and grows.

I can handle it all I can handle it all I can handle it
all **I can handle it all** I can handle it all I can
handle it all I can handle it all I can handle it all
I can handle it all I can handle it all I can handle it all I can
handle it all I can handle it all I can handle it
all I can handle it all I can handle it all I can
handle it all I can handle it all I can handle it all
II can handle it all I can handle it all I can handle it
all I can handle it all I can handle it all I can
handle it all **I can handle it all** I can handle it all
I can handle it all I can handle it all I can handle it all I can
handle it all I can handle it all I can handle it
all I can handle it all I can handle it all I can
handle it all I can handle it all I can handle it all
I can handle it all I can handle it all I can handle it
all I can handle it all I can handle it all I can
handle it all I can handle it all I can handle it all
I can handle it all **I can handle it all** I can handle it all I can
handle it all I can handle it all I can handle it
all I can handle it all I can handle it all I can
handle it all I can handle it all I can handle it all
I can handle it all I can handle it all I can handle it
all I can handle it all I can handle it all I can
handle it all I can handle it all **I can handle it all**
I can handle it all I can handle it all I can handle it all I can
handle it all I can handle it all I can handle it
all I can handle it all I can handle it all I can
handle it all I can handle it all I can handle it all
I can handle it all I can handle it all I can handle it
all I can handle it all I can handle it all I can
handle it all I can handle it all I can handle it all
I can handle it all I can handle it all I can handle it all I can
handle it all I can handle it all I can handle it
all **I can handle it all** I can handle it all I can
handle it all I can handle it all I can handle it all

Chapter 9

TO TRUST AND BE TRUSTED

The bigger your life, the smaller your fear.
—SUSAN JEFFERS

While there are many issues that involve trust in a relationship, I want to focus on the biggest trust-buster there is—the discovery that our mate is having an affair. I don't know of anything that can destroy the fabric of a relationship more quickly than that shocking discovery. And for good reason: In our Western world, it is considered the ultimate betrayal by a loved one … a blow to the heart. "How could he/she?"

Yes, how could he/she? A good question! People have affairs for all kinds of reasons: the need to prove they are desirable, unsatisfactory sex in their relationship, growing apart from their mate instead of growing together, and children who get in the way of intimacy, to name a few of them. The bottom line is that *an affair is an escape from problems we are unwilling to face within ourselves and/or within our relationship.*

By the way, don't buy into the popular myth that it is primarily a male trait to stray while it is a female trait to nest. In today's world, it seems that having extramarital affairs is not a "gender thing"; rather it's an "equal opportunity thing." As women have moved out into the world, the percentage of female extramarital affairs has equaled, and in some studies surpassed, the percentage of male affairs. I guess we don't come from different planets after all! Today's statistics are that, give or take a few percentage points, 50 percent of men have affairs, 50 percent of men don't; 50 percent of women have affairs, 50 percent don't.

Given the above, the big question that most of us—men and women alike—have asked ourselves at one time or another is: *"Can we trust our mate to be one of the 50 percent who are faithful?* While I wish I had an answer, in truth, there really is no answer: Maybe we can trust our mate; maybe we can't. Who can predict the future? Who can predict the behavior of another person? No one.

I know we all would like to have a guarantee. Unfortunately, there are no guarantees as to what our mate will or will not do. (Or, for that matter, what we will or will not do.) But when it comes to trust, I actually do have a guarantee of a different kind—*the ultimate guarantee*—and that is:

**The only thing we can safely trust is our
ability to handle what anyone ever does to us.**

I know it may not seem so at this very moment, but I have just given you great news. I have just given you the pathway to peace of mind. You no longer have to worry whether or not your mate can be trusted; your focus now is to build your own sense of power and love so that you have a deep "knowing" that whatever happens, you'll handle it. When you build up your sense of trust in yourself, the fear goes away. And when your fear goes away, you can relate to your mate in a much more loving way—of course making the likelihood of his/her having an affair much lower. It all makes sense, doesn't it?

I know that many experts talk about the importance of having total trust in our mate. Yes, a certain level of trust is good. After all, why would we want to be with someone who is an obvious "fidelity risk?"One man I know of found his fiancée in their bed with another man a few weeks before their marriage—unbelievably, he married her! But I think many experts are pointing us in the wrong direction. Much more valuable than trusting our mate is knowing that we can deal with whatever happens, and this includes the possibility of him/her being unfaithful. This level of self-trust allows harmony and flow instead of suspicion and jealousy. And, once again, it allows us to relate to our mate in a more loving way, which is a definite step in encouraging faithfulness—on both our parts! It is less likely that we or our mate will stray when there is closeness and caring right in our own home.

There are some very effective tools for building this self-trust, many of which are included in this and my previous books. Let me remind you of a few of them and how important they are in the context of building trust, whether it has to do with infidelity or any other matters involving trusting your mate:

1) **Create a rich, balanced life for yourself.** As you learned in Chapter 5, a rich, full life assures us that if any one part of our life is in disarray, the hole in our heart isn't as large. Having a rich, full life is one of the biggest protections against being emotionally devastated if our mate has an affair.

   It is important to fill your life with good friends, a sense of contribution to the community, satisfying work, hobbies you enjoy and much appreciation for all the good in your life. Most importantly, we have to commit 100 percent to each of these areas, knowing we count.

We must build in ourselves the absolute understanding that OUR LIFE IS HUGE! With our rich, full life, we say to ourselves:

> My mate is a very important part of my life, but he/she is not my whole life. I trust that he/she has my best interests at heart. I also trust that if I lose this relationship for any reason, I will go on to have a rich and beautiful life.

I suggest you repeat this statement over and over again. Soon you will feel a sense of peace. With this sense of peace, the neediness disappears and your ability to relax and love your mate with freedom and joy is enhanced—which, of course, helps to keep both of you faithful in every way.

2) ***Remember the power of affirmations***. You will recall that an affirmation is a strong positive statement that, when repeated often enough, can replace the negativity in the mind. When I begin repeating one of my favorite affirmations over and over again, I can feel my body relax and my heart swell. When it comes to the issues of trusting ourselves to handle whatever happens in our lives, the following are a couple of my favorites:

> **I let go and trust that it's all happening perfectly.**
> **I stand tall and take responsibility for my life.**
> **I am creating a beautiful love.**

Powerful statements such as these, if repeated over and over again, will take away your fear and give you a sense of peace. The key is to repeat them often enough—for example ten times in the morning and ten times at night—until they float around in your head like music. Again, what you

142

are attempting to do is replace the negative thoughts in your mind that cause fear with positive thoughts that offer peace of mind and confidence in the future.

3) *Let go of outcomes.* We enter a relationship with the hope of "till death us do part." But it doesn't always work out that way. We don't have to look any further than the divorce statistics … or the number of break-ups among committed unmarried couples. To help us deal with whatever the future holds, we have to remember to let go of our expectations, that is, to "un-set" our hearts. We do the best we can in all things, but again we have to regularly remind ourselves that:

Whatever happens, I can handle it!

It is only a heart that is set on something that is easily broken. When we un-set our heart, we are free to deal with whatever happens in our relationship … or in our lives … in a life-affirming way. Again, as we feel more powerful, we worry less and less as to what the future holds.

These are just a few fear-less tools to get you started. I suggest you read *Feel the Fear and Do It Anyway, Feel the Fear and Beyond,* and *Embracing Uncertainty* to learn more.

"Susan, what would you do if you found out your husband was having an affair?" Good question. First, let me give you a little background. In my first marriage, both my ex-husband and I had affairs. I attribute this to our being young, stupid, needy, insecure and living primarily in our Lower Selves. We had a lot to learn! I certainly have no intention of being unfaithful in my present marriage. I've grown up a lot since my first marriage and realize the intense pain that having an affair causes. I wouldn't want to cause Mark or myself such pain.

Which brings me to your question: "What would I do if I found out that Mark was having an affair?" Although one never knows for sure what one would do in the future, my answer today is that I would most likely leave the relationship. I want to be— and be with—someone who chooses to live primarily in the Higher Self and who honors his commitments. An affair would signify that his inappropriate needs had gotten in the way of his loving me, and I would leave—with love. This isn't to say that I wouldn't be brokenhearted at the beginning. I am, after all, human. But I trust I would get to the other side and go on to live a beautiful life.

I'm sure you know, as I do, those who have chosen differently. Faced with such a situation, they have chosen to stay together and work on the relationship. And some are very successful in their efforts. Usually these couples never go back to the way it was; they begin anew and slowly work on the issues that created the infidelity to begin with. With work, very successful results are possible. Ultimately, after the anger and hurt have been worked through, they have been able to make their marriage work beautifully.

And still others have stayed together under conditions that make very little sense to me. I recently learned of a woman who discovered that her husband of over twenty years had been unfaithful for most of those years. What a shock! He thought his infidelity would never be discovered, and he claimed it was never his idea to hurt her. I ask you, "How could he not be hurting her by having affairs for most of their long marriage?" In any case, she bought his story and has chosen to stay in the relationship. She feels that to forgive is very noble. I agree that forgiving is very noble ... and necessary—*but forgiving doesn't mean you have to stay in a relationship that is based on betrayal.* Time will tell if the relationship will work or not.

I suspect that many people who stay in such a relationship may be staying not out of love, but out of fear of leaving because:

"I won't find anyone else."
"He/She is such a good catch."
"I'm afraid to be alone."
"I can't afford to leave."

And so on. Obviously these individuals need to build up their trust in themselves so that their decision to stay is based on a healthy rather than an unhealthy reason. Accepting the unacceptable is death to the soul. It is so important to forgive, but you don't have to stay with a person who doesn't deserve your love.

If you are someone who has discovered your mate has strayed, here are a few suggestions as to how to keep your feelings of betrayal at bay whether you decide to walk out the door or whether you decide to stay and give the relationship another chance:

- Focus on the good that was there. So many people say, "I wasted all those years!" Obviously it was not all bad. It's only a waste if you don't focus on the good that was there.

- Work on letting go of the anger. It's understandable for anger, often rage, to be there for a little while, but don't let it ruin your life. It helps to heal our anger by focusing on the fact that our mates are human and don't always act lovingly when their own insecurities get in the way. They are doing the best they can and sometimes they make mistakes. With this understanding, we can keep our hearts open. That doesn't mean we need to stay in the relationship; it only means that we can leave with love in our hearts. (I've seen too many stay with hate in their hearts. Ugh.)

- If you decide to leave, realize that you have an opportunity to build a new and rich life for yourself. If you decide to stay, realize that you have an opportunity to learn more about love within the context of the relationship. In either case, pick up the mirror and see what part you played in the breakdown of the relationship, not to punish yourself but to gain an understanding of what behavior you need to change in the future.

- What saves us—body, mind and soul—is the knowledge that while we love our mate, we are whole without them. There is no more freeing thought that I can think of. Of course, it takes time to fill the hole in our heart and in our life if our relationship ends, but it is incredibly empowering to know we will definitely get to the other side to love again.

- Yes, we are deeply hurt if we find out our mate has strayed. It's only after the hurt and humiliation and anger are dealt with that we can begin a new life of love, either with our present mate, with a new mate or alone. We must move forward, not look back longingly at the past. As I say in *Opening Our Hearts to Men*:

  "When we go through our pain facing backwards we are caught in the quicksand of hopelessness and longing. We want what was, not what could be. But we can't go back, no matter how hard we try. So it is better to turn around and go forward."[1]

  This is a beautiful way of controlling our reactions and not playing the role of the victim.

As we go forward, it is essential to stand tall and keep in mind our safety net:

**I trust myself to handle whatever happens in my
life in an elegant, powerful and loving way.**

It is normal to shut our heart down when someone hurts us badly, but it is a gift to ourselves to be able to open our heart to that other person as time goes on. That doesn't mean that we have to stay with them in the relationship. It only means that we look beneath their hurtful behavior and understand that they are people, who, for whatever reason, don't know how to be true to themselves—or true to you.

Now let's look at the other side of the equation. What if *you* are the person tempted to have an affair? Hmm. Obviously you don't know how to be true to yourself or to your mate either. And there is also the risk of being infected by (and passing on) the HIV virus and other sexually transmitted diseases. Such a huge betrayal of our commitment to our mate can't make us feel very good about ourselves. Clearly this is a situation in which our own needs are getting in the way of love.

Unfortunately, when cheating is on our mind, many of us tend to blame our mate:

> "He/she doesn't make me feel special any more."
> "He/she isn't attractive to me any more."
> "He/she is working all the time."
> "He/she doesn't understand me."

And so it goes. Maybe all of this is true; however, an affair isn't the answer. *Dealing with the problem is the answer.* Again, your mirror will always lead you in the right direction. Trust me when I tell you that as you work to build closeness in the relationship, the temptation for either of you to have an affair will become virtually non-existent. Of course, we all could go "ooh" and "aah" when we see a member of the opposite sex who is attractive, but it is unlikely that we will violate the trust of our mate if we are in a close and intimate relationship. At least, that has been my experience with Mark. Actually the best solution is to put the "oohs" and "aahs" in your own relationship so that there is no desire on the part of either of you to stray.

Finally, if the thought of having an affair happens to cross your mind, it is important to pick up the mirror and ask yourself, "How would I feel if my mate had an affair?" Your answer should lead you in the right direction.

LOVE LESSONS

1) *Increase the Odds.* Yes, we can stray. Our mates can stray. To increase the chances of fidelity, we need to work very hard to create a delicious environment so both of us are less tempted to stray. It stands to reason that if we are angry, judgmental, self-absorbed and uncaring, our partner will be tempted to stray. If the shoe were on the other foot, wouldn't we be tempted to stray? We improve the odds considerably by creating an enthusiastic, warm, caring and wonderful environment when we are with our partner. Keep in mind, however, that even if we do our best to be loving, our mate may have an affair anyway. It happens sometimes. But, again, as we build our strength, we know that, one way or the other, we can handle it all.

2) *Review the Love Lessons in Chapter 5.* They are all relevant here. Here's a shortened version:

• Make the Higher Self mantra a part of your life: "It's all happening perfectly. Whatever happens in my life, I'll handle it. I'll learn from it. I'll grow from it. I'll make it a triumph!"

• Don't lose yourself in a relationship; and if you are already lost, find yourself again. One way to do this is by creating a rich, balanced life for yourself so that the absence of any part of your life doesn't wipe you out.

• Up-level your control addictions to preferences. Yes, we prefer our mate to be faithful, but if he/she strays, we will find a way to handle it all! That's your guarantee!

I love you I love you I love you I love you I love you I love
you I love you I love you I love you I love you I love you I
love you I love you I love you I love you I love you I love you
I love you I love you I love you I love you I love you I love
you I love you I love you I love you I love you I love you I
love you I love you I love you I love you I love you I love you
I love you I love you I love you I love you I love you I love
you I love you I love you I love you I love you I love you I
love you I love you I love you I love you I love you I love you
I love you I love you I love you I love you I love you I love
you I love you I love you I love you I love you I love you I
love you I love you I love you I love you I love you I love you
I love you I love you I love you I love you I love you I love
you I love you I love you I love you I love you I love you I
love you I love you I love you I love you I love you I love you
I love you I love you I love you I love you I love you I love
you I love you I love you I love you I love you I love you I
love you I love you I love you I love you I love you I love you
I love you I love you I love you I love you I love you I love
you I love you I love you I love you I love you I love you I
love you I love you I love you I love you I love you I love you
I love you I love you I love you I love you I love you I love
you I love you I love you I love you I love you I love you I
love you I love you I love you I love you I love you I love you
I love you I love you I love you I love you I love you I love
you I love you I love you I love you I love you I love you I
love you I love you I love you I love you I love you I love you
I love you I love you I love you I love you I love you I love
you I love you I love you I love you I love you I love you I
love you I love you I love you I love you I love you I love you
I love you I love you I love you I love you I love you I love
you I love you I love you I love you I love you I love you I

Chapter 10

THE KEY TO NEVER-ENDING SEX

Sex is one of the nine reasons for reincarnation.
The other eight are unimportant.
—HENRY MILLER

For many, sex is one of the big delights in a relationship. But for many others, sex is not a delight; it's a disappointment. Those who experience sexual dissatisfaction often suffer in silence. They don't like to admit to problems in what they consider to be an important area of their relationship. And what are some of these problems? Some women have trouble reaching an orgasm. And some men have trouble maintaining an erection. There is a great deal of incompatibility, such as one partner wanting sex much more than the other partner. Often life steps in and exhaustion becomes a factor. Children take away our privacy and energy and who has the time? And on and on. If sex is a problem in your relationship, I trust the following will spark up your love life considerably.

151

Let me begin at the beginning. Our first sexual encounters with our mate are often driven by an intense physical attraction. It's what husband and wife psychology team Judith Sherven and James Sneichowski call "skyrocket sex!"[1] One thing I can guarantee you is that this kind of lustful "I-can't-keep-my-hands-off-you" sex with your mate will not live forever. (Re-read Chapter 1.) It can, however, slowly evolve into a new and wonderful kind of sex, one that comes about as a result of a growing intimacy and a deep commitment to love one another.

So much has been written—and is still to be written—about sex. Thousands of books, legions of magazine articles and now the vast resources of the Internet are available to provide advice to singles and marrieds alike as to how to improve their sex lives, satisfy their mate beyond their wildest imaginations and experiment with the latest sexual fads and devices. While this advice is definitely titillating and can sometimes spice up one's sex life for the better, it usually has little to do with the essence of lasting love—and lasting sex. The missing ingredients are true intimacy and a loving heart.

True intimacy allows us to love "till death us do part" the sound of his/her voice, the feel of his/her touch and everything else that creates a satisfying sexual experience. You can see that a beautiful sex life is very much a reflection of the total picture of your love for one another. I might add that there are many relationships where sex is not an issue because you and your mate have worked out a basis for a loving and fulfilling partnership where neither one of you requires sex. But I'll wager that most happy and enduring relationships revolve to some degree around an enjoyable sex life. As relationship expert Michele Weiner-Davis says:

"Sex is an extremely important part of marriage. When it's good, it offers couples opportunities to give and receive physical pleasure, to connect emotionally and spiritually. It builds closeness, intimacy, and a sense of partnership. It defines their relationship as different from all others. Sex is a powerful tie that binds."[2]

Our experience of sex in a relationship is always transforming into new and hopefully more intimate forms. After the blissful enchantment of early love, sex ultimately comes down to earth to become familiar and what some people call "routine." While there is an assumption that "routine" sex is boring and uninteresting, trust me when I tell you it doesn't have to be that way.

The word "routine" is usually defined in two ways: 1) boring and 2) a ritual. If we keep routine on the side of "a ritual" instead of "boring," we can have a truly wonderful experience. The rituals of loving sex are delicious. This is because, after a while, a couple hopefully whittles away what doesn't work and is left with what is most enjoyable in the sex act. And it is this "most enjoyable" that becomes routine sex. What possibly could be wrong with that?

In fact, so much that is "routine" about a loving relationship in general are the special moments—the special rituals we come to treasure: cuddling at night, sitting down to dinner, eating at our favorite restaurant, watching our favorite television shows, and the way we make love. Put all these rituals (routines) together and you have the essence of a beautiful life together. So let's dispel this erroneous notion that "routine" is necessarily bad. It can be the stuff out of which fantastic relationships are made.

This doesn't mean that little variations in the sex act can't be introduced to titillate, but they don't have to be big variations. It is delicious to extend the boundaries just a small fraction. Tiny adjustments in your position, where you place your hands or arms or legs, the way you breathe or blow on his/her body, a small shift in the way you kiss—the adjustments of pleasure. When you are in the throes of lovemaking and you are both experiencing the passion that this wonderful intimacy provides, every nuance and every subtle movement can make a difference in heightening your own and your mate's pleasure. These minute, physical adjustments

The Feel the Fear Guide to Lasting Love

to your lovemaking compound over time to make the act of love better and better and better.

It goes without saying (but I'm saying it anyway) we have to tell our partner what brings us pleasure. If there is something bothering you regarding your sexual relationship, you have an obligation, in the interests of true intimacy, to say something about it in a loving way. Minor problems related to technique can be easily fixed and there is no reason for not dealing with them. *Your partner is not a mind-reader.* He/she can't possibly know if something doesn't—or does—feel good for you unless you tell him/her.

Most men and women would love it if their partners expressed what feels good in a sexual way. Many men and women simply don't know how their partner's body works. And let the secret be told … we are all different! There are no books that can tell you what ALL MEN and ALL WOMEN find satisfying. Women talking together express many differences regarding what they find sexually satisfying. Men talking together express many differences regarding what they find sexually satisfying. As a result, we have to let our partner know what is particularly satisfying to us … and, just as importantly, we have to ask them what is satisfying to them. We aren't mind-readers either.

Our mates may feel embarrassed to tell us what does and doesn't work for them, so ask them. "Does this feel good? Tell me what you like best." As you learn more and more about what pleases your partner, and he/she learns more about what pleases you, sex can become very satisfying indeed.

One of the problems that we all have regarding sex is that life gets in the way and it is one of the first things to go in a busy life. This is a pity since, if it is good, sex is the glue that helps a relationship to stay whole. Not to worry, I have the perfect solution:

PUT SEX ON YOUR TO-DO LIST!

Make it a permanent entry in your calendar. *Scheduling sex helps to assure sex.* Let me show you how this works. If you have to rise early, work hard all day and are very tired at night, sex isn't usually what you have in mind as you both climb into bed. A hug, a kiss, a thank you and a touch are all beautiful and a valuable part of saying good night, but often sex is not on the agenda. In this case, you might be a perfect candidate for scheduling sex as a weekend pleasure. This means setting a time on the weekend when the order of the day is SEX. I will admit to you now (but don't tell anyone) that Mark and I schedule sex on Saturday and Sunday mornings. Our friends and family already are alerted to this fact. And the phone never rings before 11 a.m.

I know you are wondering, "Isn't spontaneous sex better … having sex when the mood hits you?" Of course, spontaneous sex is exciting. But, as I've already explained, after many years in a relationship, the uncontrollable urge to jump into bed every time you look at one another usually diminishes … and sometimes even disappears. But there is something beautiful you can introduce in its stead … and that is a "ritual of love." For Mark and me, it looks like this:

> Saturday morning arrives. Whoever gets up first makes the coffee and brings it and the newspaper into bed. We appreciate and often note to each other how wonderful these times together are. At some point in time, we take a shower together, and I put on my special "love" potion, a special fragrance that I wear only when we make love. It has become an aphrodisiac for both of us! We come back to bed … and you'll have to imagine the rest. Heaven! When we have done the delicious deed, we cuddle up and just hold each other and thank each other for such marvelous pleasure.

You may be thinking, "That sounds great, Susan. But what if you are not in the mood?" Aha! A very important question. There definitely are times when I'm not in the mood. There definitely are times when Mark is not in the mood. But for both of us, it only takes a few minutes of touching in all the right places to absolutely get in a sexy and delicious mood! If you think about it, a mood can be changed very easily when it comes to sex. Start with a gentle kiss ... a gentle touch ... the words, I love you ... mmm. Need I say more.

If you are not turned on to sex at any given moment and your partner is, it helps to say to yourself, "I may not be in the mood at this moment, but I want to give my mate pleasure." And, again, it doesn't take long to get in the mood. So now you can take "I'm not in the mood" off your list of reasons not to have sex. Of course, all of us have times when, for various reasons, we have to say no to sex—illness, trauma in the family, stress, exhaustion and the like. But, generally speaking, getting in the mood for sex is very easy to do.

You may be thinking, "That sounds great, Susan. But what if you have children?" Yes, you've already learned that children, cute and cuddly as they are, can mess up your sex life. My favorite quote relative to sex and children comes from television writer and producer Geoff Deane:

"On the odd occasion that you can both muster up the energy you will discover that nature has installed a modem connecting the man's erection to his son's lungs. You get a hard-on and he starts to cry. Soon the moment has passed and so has your boner. What have you done to deserve this?"[3]

The following quotes are from two women I interviewed when writing *I'm Okay ... You're a Brat:*

"I felt like I'd been a prisoner for five months ... a stinky one at that. Who had the time or energy to take a shower or wash my hair? I was pathetic. And this child of mine spent its life pooping and peeing and spitting up all over my shirt. My breasts were so sore and scabby that I wanted to scream. Sex? Are you crazy?"[4]

"I don't need to go to the gym. I am lugging, schlepping, and running all day. Then I'm exhausted. Sex has gone out the window. Anyone who says they are having sex with little kids around is lying. Totally lying. Who has the energy? It's hard to think about sex when you are changing a diaper or the baby is spitting up on your shirt. My husband is exhausted also. What a team!"[5]

One woman, thankfully, took a more hopeful approach to the situation—one that if you have children, you might be well-served adopting:

"I look forward to great sex when the kids are gone. My husband and I work on keeping enough passion and playfulness and rapport. Nobody's angry at the other. I feel parents are pressured to believe that if they are not having sex like they did before, something is wrong. Not necessarily. It's just how it is. It goes with the territory. I think it's something to think about before you have kids. Nobody tells you your sex life will wane. But even if they were told, people don't believe it will happen to them. I wonder why they think that."[6]

Yes, we can take a positive approach to the inevitable lessening of our sex life once a child is born. But even with a child, we can be creative. We can find a way to get away from the kids regularly for a romantic interlude to experience the sexual intimacy that certainly does a relationship good.

Remember that your relationship with your mate is your priority. Ultimately the children will leave home, and it is important to keep your relationship healthy and happy. If you have broken your connection with your mate, home can be a very lonely place once the children go off to live their own lives. So creativity is the order of the day. Even with children, find ways to keep the home-fires burning.

Speaking of the children growing up and leaving home, I have some really good news for you:

Aging and sex absolutely DO go together … beautifully!

Not only does age NOT signal the end of sex, it actually may improve it! "Susan, how can that be?" Well, think about it. When the kids leave home, you have more time and privacy. The two of you are as you began—alone together. Your life is lighter and, hopefully, less stressful in many ways. More time, more privacy … heaven. And your sex life can go on for a very, very long time.

I learned my lesson about sex and aging when I was relatively young. In my thirties, I became the executive director of The Floating Hospital, known as New York's Ship of Health. A number of weeks of the year were devoted to senior citizens, and the average age of the people who came aboard was seventy-five. My staff and I decided that we should have a class for the elderly about dating, since so many of them had lost their spouses.

On my staff was a very talented puppeteer who devised a gentle little puppet show depicting two elderly puppet-people dancing and talking about their love. They both had lost their spouses and were happy to find love again. Then in walks the man's puppet-son who, because he is loyal to his deceased mother, is appalled to see his father dancing with a new woman. The rest of the skit was about the man explaining to his son his need for love and warmth. And the play ended with the boy and his father embracing. Sweet.

At that point, the subject of dating was opened up for discussion. The first question was from a man sitting in the back of the room. I was a bit taken aback when he asked in a very loud voice, "How do I get it up and make it stay up?" A shock wave went through our young staff. It was inconceivable to them that people of this age were even *thinking* about sex! The shockwaves increased when a little old lady—and I kid you not—with white gloves and a flowery frock gently raised her hand and said, "My boyfriend just does it and turns over and goes to sleep. Do you have any suggestions as to how I can make it more satisfying for me?"

Yes, we were shocked, but it was a very pleasant shock. It was nice to learn that sex doesn't have to end with aging. Interestingly, the British charity, Age Concern, is encouraging elderly couples to have an active sex life in order to stay healthy. They teach that regular sex can make the elderly feel younger, reduce stress, boost self-esteem and lead to a better night's sleep. They publish a book by Dr. Sarah Brewer, who writes:

"Physical intimacy doesn't fizzle out and disappear as you get older. When you enjoy a rewarding and regular sex life, all aspects of life, including the enormous range of benefits to your health, tend to take on a rosier hue."[7]

You have to admit, the news gets better and better! We have long believed that men enjoy a healthy sex life well into their senior years, but writer Jonathan Margolis reports that:

"Not only are women having sex into their eighties, but there is a growing belief that they are built to enjoy sex and orgasms more as they get older."[8]

I like that. But why is he limiting it to women in their eighties I have found evidence that many enjoy it well into their nineties. Wow! It's certainly great to know you have the possibility of a long sex-life ahead of you. Margolis also tells us:

"Behavioural and attitudinal research findings are remarkable, proving that older women have fuller sex lives than their younger counterparts."

He attributes this to the fact that many older women "are freed from pregnancy concerns, guilt, periods, financial worries, career stress and tiredness, which render up to seventy percent of young women in the urban West uninterested in sex." This comment makes you look forward to aging!

I have a theory: If you loved sex as a younger person, you will love sex as an older person. My husband is happy that I loved sex as a younger person, and I am definitely loving it now in my sixties—and I expect to enjoy it for many years to come. If you didn't love sex as a younger person, you would be wise to learn how to love sex as an older person. It's never too late!

"Okay, Susan," I hear you ask, "that's all well and good, but what if your mate—young or old—just isn't interested?" Hmm. Yes, there is a problem when you are ready and willing but your partner isn't. Again, the myth prevails that men want sex more than women. I haven't seen any evidence of that. Some men do; some men don't. In fact, one of the chief complaints of many women is that their mate has lost interest in sex. One young woman said, "My husband and I want to have a child, but I don't know how my husband thinks this is going to happen when he has no interest in sex!" Good question.

If your partner is no longer interested in sex, first talk about it. Ask if he/she is angry about something. Or overwhelmed with life. Ask if there is something you can do to make him/her more interested in sex. If talking doesn't work, couple counseling may help. Love Lesson #3 that follows offers some more suggestions. It is certainly worth the effort to do everything you can to make sex a wonderfully enjoyable and meaningful part of your relationship. Make it an adventure in learning—and in pleasure.

LOVE LESSONS

1) *Keep yourself on the side of love.* Let me once again refer to the Love Chart I presented in Chapter 7. There is nothing that destroys a sexual appetite for your mate more than anger, resentment and criticism. When anger, resentment and criticism rule the roost, you can't stand the way he/she eats, let alone the feel of his/her touch! Sex killers, indeed! Anger, criticism and resentment may increase your own or your mate's appetite for *extramarital* sex, but if you want lasting sex on the homefront, anger, criticism and resentment certainly have to go! The more you move yourself in the direction of love, the more likely it is that your love affair with your mate will grow and grow.

When the heart is loving sex is pure joy. It has been said that the main sexual organ is the brain. Sex also involves our emotions. If we are angry, if we are insecure, if we are resentful, if we are unhappy, sex truly suffers. If we are happy, loving, caring, and strong, sex can truly thrive. So move yourself in the direction of love so that your sexual relationship can thrive.

2) *TOUCH ... TOUCH ... TOUCH.* Touching is an essential part of an enduring relationship. Relationship experts Douglas and Naomi Moseley have this to say about it:

"No amount of insight or understanding of deeper issues will be of any use in enhancing sexuality unless a couple is willing to give and receive touch on a regular basis."[9]

They go on to recommend that partners should touch each other for at least ten minutes each day. Sounds good to me! Touching in any form is great. Give him/her a hug when he/she walks out the door. When walking down the street, hold hands. One woman reported that when she and her boyfriend are together, he often will grab her bum and say something loving like: "You've got the most beautiful bum in the world." She said that she likes when he says this, even if it's true only for him, because it makes her feel physically desired, a beautiful feeling indeed. So touch, touch, touch. Make your mate feel desired, desirable and, ultimately, desirous. Delicious.

3) *Seek help if there are problems.* There are two obvious places to seek help when sex is a problem:

- **Your local sex shop.** Yes, your local sex shop. A dear friend of mine, Joy Starr, owns a sex shop. (Her name was Joy long before she opened the sex shop!) Joy was one of my original *Feel the Fear and Do It Anyway* students. Obviously, she felt the fear and opened a sex shop anyway! Joy works with her daughter Shana. They both love what they are doing because they are able to help so many people improve their sex lives. They see the shop as a valuable source of important and accurate information. They even are invited to teach classes about sex by the neighboring universities. They have helped young and old get in touch with their sexual selves.

  Joy and Shana report that many men and women, young and old, come in to seek help for their significant others, who for one reason or other are not able to enjoy sex. Sometimes couples come in together to seek help. Some just phone, too embarrassed to talk about their problems in person. Joy and Shana say their role is to guide them and give them reliable information. They are very proud of what they are doing since they have been able to educate so many as to the magic of sex. I suspect the men and women they have helped are eternally grateful.[10]

  Of course, it is doubtful that this kind of service and expertise is available in most local sex shops, but it is worth a visit to investigate what is available to help you and your partner better enjoy sex in your relationship.

- **Consult your doctor.** Many sexual problems have their roots in physiological difficulties. If things are awry physically, a reduced desire for sex is very common. In addition, certain medications can really put a damper on your sex life. There are solutions to many of the physical problems that plague our sexual lives, so don't feel embarrassed to tell your doctor what the problem is.

4) *Keep yourself healthy ... and sexy.* Love is not blind. Very often our looks decline unnecessarily once we are in a relationship—not out of age but out of neglect. We gain weight and we don't care how we look. It is important once again to pick up the mirror, but this time, not to look inside but to look "outside" to see where we need some physical improvement. I feel the emphasis on looks is certainly too strong in our society, but an emphasis on health is a good thing. Usually, the better our health, the better we look, the better we feel about ourselves and the better our mate will feel about us. To keep your love alive, keep your body alive with nourishment, exercise, a happy attitude and all good things.

5) *Keep the electricity flowing.* Flirting is never out of style and it is a great way to keep the electricity flowing between you and your mate. Flirting takes many forms; sexy chatter, sexy love notes, sexy e-mails and the like all keep the electricity—and the love—flowing. So never stop the play that flirting allows. It's your opportunity to lighten up, have fun and create a sense of play. And it is certainly a way to enhance the electricity that makes love glow.

thank you for being in my life thank you for being in my life thank you for being in my life thank you for being in my life thank you for being in my life thank you for being in my life thank you for being in my life thank you for being in my life thank you for being in my life thank you for being in my life thank you for being thank you for being in my life thank you for being in my life thank you for being in my life thank you for being in life thank you for being in my life thank you for being in my life thank you for being in my life thank you for being thank you for being in my life thank you for being in my life thank you for being in my life thank you for being in life thank you for being in my life thank you for being in my life thank you for being in my life thank you for being thank you for being in my life thank you for being in my life thank you for being in my life thank you for being in life thank you for being in my life thank you for being in my life thank you for being in my life thank you for being in my life thank you for being in my life thank you for being thank you for being in my life thank you for being in my life thank you for being in my life thank you for being in life thank you for being in my life thank you for being in my life thank you for being in my life thank you for being in my life thank you for being in my life thank you for being in my life thank you for being in my life thank you for being in my life thank you for being in my life thank you for being in my life thank you for being in life thank you for being in my life thank you for being in my life thank you for being in my life thank you for being in my life thank you for being in my life thank you for being thank you for being in my life thank you for being in my life thank you for being in my life thank you for being in life thank you for being in my life thank you for being in my life thank you for being in my life thank you for being thank you for being in my life thank you for being

Chapter 11

THE SOUND OF LOVE

We can learn that the essence of love is not to use the other to make us happy but to serve and affirm the one we love. And we can discover, to our surprise, that what we have needed more than anything was not so much to be loved, as to love.
—ROBERT JOHNSON[1]

It was exciting news. Mark's son was getting married and Mark was asked to be the best man. He knew that, as is customary, he would be called upon to give a little talk. For months prior to the wedding, he thought about what special advice he could give to send the bride and groom on the pathway toward a wonderful life together.

The time finally came for him to deliver his talk, and the words that came out of his mouth were moving, funny and wise. But what created a very special moment for the entire room was when he gave the bride and groom the seven magical words that they were to say to each other daily. And these words were:

"Thank you for being in my life."

Certainly all the guests at the wedding were very moved. At the end of Mark's talk, as everyone stood and began toasting the bride and groom and each other, you could hear the words, "Thank you for being in my life" reverberating throughout the room, accompanied by a tangible sense of love and appreciation. Mark spoke from experience, because these are the words that continue to bring a feeling of blessing into our hearts as we, in our own marriage, repeat them daily.

The deeply important words, "thank you," represent a monumentally grand way to celebrate love. Yet, for a number of unfortunate reasons, they are words too seldom spoken. Anger and resentment often get in the way, and we would rather bite our tongue than utter the simple but priceless words, "thank you." As psychologist Howard Markman reminds us:

> "The simple reality is that most of us are the least honoring of those we love the most. We get frustrated, angry, or disappointed, and off we go, talking to this person we love the most in ways that don't seem very loving at all."[2]

Yes, some of us, consciously or unconsciously, withhold our expression of love, thanks and appreciation and, sadly, express disapproval instead. When I think of my first marriage, I can't remember saying "thank you" for much, even though my then-husband was a man who was very giving. Instead, I was in the critical mode. I certainly noticed the things I didn't like, and constantly let him know. I can guarantee that this lack of appreciation and thanks is death to love … and death to the soul.

I remember conducting a thirteen week workshop for women. One of the assignments was to go home and thank their mates. They were not happy about this assignment. You would have thought I'd asked them to go home and burn down their houses! One woman immediately responded by saying, "*He* should be happy *I'm* there." I asked, "Why are you there?" She was taken aback, thought for a moment and said, "I don't want to be alone." I said, "Fine. That's a good start. Go home and thank him for being in your life."

When the women came back the following week, they were shocked at how difficult it was for them to thank their mates, even those who thought of themselves as very loving. Prior to that time, they had never even noticed their lack of appreciation! Some realized that they were angry and resentful; some did not feel appreciated themselves ... and on it went. One woman gave an interesting reason for not saying thank you. She said:

> "My husband does so much for me, and I'm grateful for it all. But I never tell him, and when I asked myself why, the answer I got was that I am pretending to be independent—to look like I'm independent. If he gives me so much, how am I independent?"

Hmm. She hasn't learned that independence has very little to do with appreciation of the many gifts we are given every day of our lives. True independence is the inner knowledge that, "Whatever happens, I'll handle it!" Ironically, one of the ways we "handle it" is to notice and appreciate all the gifts we are given. Aha! When I told her this, a lightbulb went on in her head. She got it!

The good news is that all the women in the group determined that they would deal with their resistance and become ever watchful and appreciative of all the good that their mates brought into their life. We worked on this throughout the workshop, and it transformed their whole energy when it came to their relationships: Appreciation caused their anger to diminish and their love to grow. More than that, I watched them become more beautiful people. The look of anger and resentment is off-putting; the look of love is very attractive!

We all need to learn how to be watchful and appreciative. Too many of us withhold our thanks for the simple reason that we fail to notice the many things our mate does for us. So much is taken for granted. Consciousness of all the beauty that our mate brings into our lives is an important ingredient of lasting love … and a beautiful life. By definition:

**The more we say "thank you"
the more we feel our abundance.**

The words "thank you" mean we have been given something. If we say these words often enough, any trace of a poverty consciousness disappears, and we begin feeling incredibly abundant. We focus on what is there, not on what isn't.

It stands to reason that by not repeatedly saying "thank you" we are hurting ourselves just as much as we are hurting the one we claim to love. Saying "thank you" is a recognition that we are taking. If we refuse to take, we feel no one is giving. Our mate can be giving us a lot, but in fact our refusal to notice and acknowledge him/her makes us feel cheated and hungry for love.

When we look deeply at the many times we forget to thank our partners for various things they have done for us, we see that it truly hurts our heart … and theirs. I learned this lesson a few years after my first marriage ended. After some time had passed, I called my ex-husband and asked if I could take him to lunch. At this very important lunch, I told him all the admirable things about him that I couldn't tell him when we were married because of my own insecurities. I talked about how giving he was, what a loving father he was, how much he had contributed to my life, and the like. He cried. I cried. And something was healed in both our hearts. This healing allowed me to go on to create the beautiful relationship I now have with Mark. I might add that my ex-husband and I remain loving friends today.

If you recognize yourself in any of this, it is time to open your eyes to the many gifts you are being given in your relationship and utter the simple words, "thank you." They may be among the most important you will ever utter.

And then there are the words "I love you." As I mentioned earlier, these also are such important words to say frequently in our relationship. Because of our early training, many of us have a difficult time opening up in terms of our feelings of love. You know the answer to that:

FEEL THE FEAR AND SAY
'I LOVE YOU' ANYWAY!

As I also mentioned earlier, we have to learn to recognize the love coming from our mate if he/she is incapable of verbally expressing it. The expression of love comes in many forms. It could be a husband taking a wife's car in to be inspected. It could be a wife making something special for dinner. It could be buying a special treat for our partner. When our mate does something nice, let them know: "This makes me feel very, very good. I love you and I thank you." Let them feel your love and appreciation for whatever they do for you.

In a survey conducted by Dr. Phil McGraw, 94 percent of respondents believed that giving flowers, holding hands, evenings out and the like are loving acts. Yet, interestingly, two-thirds also characterized mundane chores such as taking out the trash, bathing the kids, or doing the dishes as acts of love. Dr. McGraw concluded, "What these actions say to your mate is, *I want your life to be better, and I'll make personal sacrifices to ensure that.*"[3] In other words: "I love you."

So if you are having difficulty finding the gifts, just think of all the so-called mundane tasks that your mate does in the course of everyday life—all are expressions of his/her love and deserving of your thanks. "But, Susan, that's his/her job." I suspect that as you begin saying "I love you" and "Thank you" to your mate for doing his/her "job," it will melt his/her heart—and yours. As I pointed out in Chapter 3, as we change our own behavior, we have the capacity to change our mate's behavior as well. Remember this:

Every relationship has its good and every relationship has its bad. By focusing on the bad, we starve. By focusing on the good, we thrive … allowing us to creatively and lovingly deal with the bad!

Many of us spend much of our lives feeling sad, or angry, or depressed, or rotten or cheated. Part of the problem is that we can't see all the love we are being given. Wouldn't it be great if a red light would go on every time our mate did something wonderful for us, little things, big things: They all become expected behavior when in fact they are all *gifts*.

So begin right now by appreciating all that your mate does in your life. Don't let another moment pass before you say, "Thank you for being in my life. I love you." If he/she is in the other room, go right in and say these meaningful words. If he/she is not there, pick up the phone and call him/her. (Be thankful for cell phones.) Do it now. And do it often. Remember the beautiful words of Dale Carnegie:

> "If you and I will inspire the people with whom we come in contact to a realization of the hidden treasure they possess, we can do far more than change people. We can literally transform them."[4]

Let me now introduce you to a very special way of celebrating and enhancing your love. For those of us who are married, the sound of love includes the vows we repeated to one another during our wedding ceremony. But too often, in the course of everyday living, we forget our promise, our commitment. One of the solutions is to repeat these vows regularly. I know a couple that does it monthly. Mark and I reaffirm our wedding vows yearly, on the day of our anniversary.

Happily, when we were married those many years ago, my sister and maid of honor, held a little audio recorder that captured the entire ceremony—and beyond. I even have the sound of my mother, who died a number of years ago, exclaiming when the ceremony ended, "Beautiful! My Susie's married again." It's a vibrant reminder of the happiness my mother felt. Each year, we need only replay the audiotape and repeat, with the audiotape, the vows we said at our original wedding ceremony. It is magical.

Sometimes Mark and I say our vows to each other privately; sometimes we say them with family and friends in attendance. Sometimes we say them on the top of a mountain, on the beach, in our home, in a hotel or wherever the spirit moves us. Each time we say our vows, tears come to my eyes. I feel blessed beyond words, and our commitment to each other is lifted up just a little higher. And over more than nineteen years (as I write this) of saying our vows, it's become very high indeed!

I understand that not everyone has a recording of their vows. If this is true for you, you can re-affirm your vows by re-marrying with an actual ceremony, this time recording it all. If for any reason this is not practical for you, simply write a beautiful statement such as the following that you and your partner read to each other at regular intervals. Stand face to face and say these words to each other, one of you at a time:

I love you and I thank you. You have brought so much joy and beauty into my life. You are my love, my best friend and the person with whom I want to share my life. Having come to love you from the depth of my heart, I dedicate myself to your happiness and wellbeing. Through the bad times that life can bring, I will be there to comfort you. And through the good times, I will be there to celebrate and rejoice. In giving to you, I give to myself. The true reward of love is taking pleasure in the giving.

My commitment is to love and to cherish, to honor and trust; in adversity and prosperity, to believe in you and

to share with you all the triumphs and joys; to create a lasting union based on caring and concern; to recognize your individuality and to support you in being the very best you can be. As I focus on my many blessings, I thank you for making my life complete.

Whether you are married or not, you and your partner regularly can say this or your own statement to reaffirm your love and commitment to each other. Remember that your love for each other, like a beautiful tree, has to be watered, nurtured, loved and cared for in order for it to grow into a huge, full-blown lasting love. Regularly repeating your commitment to each other does wonders for keeping your love a priority.

The following Love Lessons will give you some further ideas for turning up the sights and sounds of love in your relationship. Pick the ones that speak to you and practice, practice, practice. Use these ideas as a springboard for creating your own celebration of your relationship.

LOVE LESSONS

1) *Expand your words of love one week at a time.* Saying words of love has to become a *habit.* Here's the plan:

Week one: At dinner, before you go to sleep at night, or whenever feels right for you, turn to your partner and say the loving words, "Thank you for being in my life." Make this a daily practice. If you have other words of thanks you would prefer to use, use them.

Week two: In addition to saying your thanks each day of the week, add the words, "I love you." For some, this may be more difficult, but it so important to the quality of your love life to make saying these words a natural flow that comes from your being. So again: *Feel the fear and say "I love you" anyway!*

Each week that follows: Add to your list of words of appreciation. For example:

I'm blessed to be with you.
You're great.
I'm really lucky to have you in my life.

Practice these words and the many others you can think of and make them a part of your vocabulary when it comes to your mate. As I have already pointed out, *not only will this make your mate feel loving toward you, it will also remind you of the blessings that your mate brings into your life.*

(Remember the concept of "act-as-if." Even if you are upset about something, act-as-if you are appreciative of all the good. If you act-as-if often enough, you actually live into the reality that there is so much good.)

2) *Talk beautifully about your mate in the company of others.* Another gem from Dale Carnegie:

"Give the other person a fine reputation to live up to."[5]

I love it! When you talk beautifully about your mate, it encourages him/her to be the best that he/she can be. We all have a hunger to be appreciated. Those who satisfy that desire in others will be loved indeed.

3) *Be who you want your partner to be.* Remember that like attracts like. Practice the qualities you wish to find in your mate. If you want love, act lovingly. If you want happiness, spread happiness. If you want appreciation, show appreciation. If you want understanding, give understanding. I love Werner Erhard's reminder that, "If love is scarce, who isn't creating it?" Hmm. It's time to create it and create it and create it. *Don't be passive when it comes to love!*

A word of advice: Give love in all its forms freely without expecting anything back. If you expect something to come back, it is barter, not giving. When you give love freely and your mate doesn't respond, keep your heart open and continue to act lovingly. Send loving light. Chances are that their heart will melt. If not, your heart will tell you what you need to do.

4) *Make time!* I'm always amazed at how busy couples spend their weekends *not* spending time together … the tennis match, going off with friends, overworking, etc. I watch so many couples squander their love by making other things more important. Your relationship needs to be your top priority. Ask yourself, "What can I let go of so I can spend more time with my love?" In their book *How to Stay in Love,* Charlie and Martha Shedd call it "dropping the good for the better."[6] I like that! Yes, there are always good things to do in life outside the marriage, but sometimes it serves

us well to "drop the good for the better." While it is important to keep our lives rich and full, sometimes it's better to let go of some of the richness out there and nourish the richness of the relationship. You have to ask yourself:

> Do I really have to go to this meeting?
> Do I really have to go to this soccer game?
> Do I really have to work today?
> Do I really have to … whatever?

Sometimes you have to; sometimes you don't. But if you keep your relationship as your highest priority, you will always find ways of finding more and more time together … even if children are involved. (See Chapter 8.)

5) **Become a romantic.** It's really important to keep in mind that love is an emotion, but just as importantly, love is an *action*. The question you need to keep asking yourself is:

"What am I doing to keep love alive?"

Action is key when romance is involved. It's also a way of keeping us conscious! We need actions that help us keep our focus on how blessed we are to have our partner in our life. What kind of actions am I talking about? I'm talking about not only words of love, but also celebrations of love with gifts, surprises and loving attention.

If your habit has been to be unconscious in your relationship, your goal is to make it a habit of paying attention and regularly showering your mate with love. If you can't think of romantic things to do to keep love alive, consult the internet for ideas. Now that so many of us are internet-savvy, it is a handy resource to teach us how to celebrate love. For example, as part of my research for writing this book, I logged onto www.Lovingyou.com

and found articles and special features, love e-cards, love dedica-tions, romantic ideas and so on. Many ideas are obvious, but too often we don't pay enough attention to the obvious:

> kisses, hugs, a bubble bath together, sending cards, love letters and loving e-mails, cuddling, mutual massages, sending a gift, planning a surprise weekend, creating a scrapbook of pictures that remind both of you of happy times, placing "I love you" cards all over, buying flowers, candle lit dinners …

Yes, the obvious is wonderful! I suggest you do one little thing in the relationship every day that will make your partner feel good. Remember that little is big! Be creative. You know your mate pretty well and you know what makes him/her feel good. Again, don't expect a particular reaction. Just do one thing daily as a way of honoring your mate and your Higher Purpose, that of becom-ing a more loving person. Again, it may take time to push through any resistance you may feel, but keep pushing. Eventually you will get to the other side.

You have to make loving actions a habit. Trust me when I tell you that a beautiful love can't exist when we take the blessings of our union for granted. So, I repeat, do one thing in the relationship every day that will make your partner feel good. Put it in your diary. In so doing you remind yourself of your good fortune of being together. Always remember that moments of love add up to a lifetime of love.

6) *Appreciate the little things.* Loving acts can be the little things. In fact, it is the little things that shape a love. The big splashes of brilliance are grand, but they don't define the essence of a loving relationship. It's the everyday that counts. For exam-ple, we had a fire in our building. I was visiting a neighbor on the 17th floor. Mark was on the 14th floor. A few seconds after the

loud speakers started announcing that we were to exit the building, in walked Mark. Instead of leaving immediately, he ran up to make sure I was all right and we walked down the 17 flights of steps together. I felt very loved. The good news is that I know I would have done the same if the situation were reversed. Of course, the fire department may think we are being very stupid, but they may not understand how much we love each other.

When on a deadline, my son-in-law works late hours. He often gets home after my daughter has gone to sleep. Before he comes to bed, he puts some toothpaste on her toothbrush and leaves it on the side of the sink ready for her when she wakes up. It's one of his many ways of saying, "I love you." And her heart sings when she finds his beautiful and creative message of love.

Remember: *There is no such thing as a little gift.* No matter how "small," it is big in its message. It says loud and clear, "I thought about you and I give you my love." It's a very big thing actually. We want to matter to each other. We have to show our loved one that they do matter. And when we are given a gift of any kind, we have to express the thanks for the caring we are being shown.

7) ***Focus on the Abundance.*** In *Feel the Fear and Do It Anyway* I introduced readers to the Book of Abundance. Let me introduce it to you here. Each night list the many wonderful things—big and small— that happened to you during the day. For example:

  1. My car started.
  2. I had a great lunch.
  3. The sun was shining.

Now, devote ample space in your Book of Abundance to the wonderful things your mate has provided you:

4. Bill gave me a big hug when I came home.
5. We had a wonderful dinner together.
6. Bill called me at work just to say hello.

By regularly listing all the beauty that your mate brings into your life, you are making appreciation of him/her a habit.

Try to make your daily list reach the number fifty ... yes, fifty. By "stretching" in this way, you learn to focus daily on all the good in your life instead of the bad. As you have learned, when we are not in the habit of appreciating, we are left with a sense of scarcity in our lives—and our relationships—instead of abundance.

8) *Remember to have patience.* As you ramp up the level of love in your relationship, it may take a little while for your mate to catch on. The key is not to expect anything in return. Remember you are learning to be a more loving person *despite what your mate is doing.* Again, there may come a time when you feel it is time to leave ... with love. In any case, each new challenge offers us an opportunity to practice ... practice ... practice how to become a more loving person.

PART III

FREEDOM TO BE
... YOU AND ME

I let go I let go I let go I let go I let go I let go I let go I let go I let go I let go **I let go** I let go **I let go** I let go **I let go** I let go **I let go** I let go I let go I let go I let go I let go I let go I let go I let go I let go I let go I let go I let go I let go I let go I let go I let go I let go I let go I let go **I let go** I let go **I let go** I let go **I let go** I let go I let go I let go I let go I let go I let go I let go I let go I let go I let go I let go I let go I let go I let go I let go I let go I let go **I let go** I let go I let go I let go I let go I let go I let go I let go I let go I let go I let go I let go I let go I let go I let go I let go I let go I let go I let go I let go **I let go** I let go I let go I let go I let go I let go I let go I let go I let go I let go I let go I

Chapter 12

_____

LOVE ON A
SHIFTING CARPET

For the first time in history, every couple is on their own
to discover how to build a healthy relationship, and to
forge their own vision of how and why to be together.
—JOHN WELWOOD[1]

Freedom! How sweet it is! Or is it? I used to have a book with
a very clever cartoon on the cover. It depicted a man looking
down in terror at a chain around his leg. The reason that he was
looking down in terror was that *someone had cut the chain ...* he
was now free! "HELP!"

In recent years, the chain has been cut from around the legs of
all of us when it comes to relationships. With few exceptions, we
are free to be whoever we want to be. We are no longer chained to
traditional roles. For many of us, this freedom is fantastic! For
many of us, however, it's very scary and incredibly confusing!
"HELP!"

It *seems* that it was much easier in my mother's time: Society told us the exact roles we were to play in our relationships. It sounded something like:

"Women, you take care of the home and the kids."
"Men, you go to work and provide for your family."

Very simple. In Western society, men and women both knew their "place" in this big wide world, limited as it was. The problem is that many of us were miserable in our confined roles. We felt trapped and unfulfilled. Those who dared to break the rules were severely criticized. It was not a happy time for many couples. These days, we all are much freer to choose different roles, and the possibilities are enormous. In today's world:

- Men stay at home and take care of the children while the women are the financial providers.

- Men and women both work and contribute equally to the household.

- Men brag about their cooking skills while women admit they are lousy cooks.

- Women give men alimony … and sometimes even give them the kids!

- Women and men play traditional roles, with her staying home and him going out to work.

- Both men and women work and decide not to have children.

- Both men and women work part-time so that each can be involved in the raising of the children.

And the possibilities go on and on.

Now what could possibly be wrong with this picture? On the surface, nothing. We've come a long, long way. But looking a little deeper, we can see that our new freedom often creates chaos and confusion within our relationships. We notice that the divorce rate is very high and we also notice that some men and women have difficulty even finding a mate.

The "good" news is that, as painful as it is, chaos and confusion are to be expected. This freedom is all relatively new. I shock younger people when I point out that when my mother was young, women in the U.S. didn't even vote. Changing the collective mindset is slow and not enough time has passed for the new shift in roles to feel comfortable and natural. Old stereotypes take a long time to die.

And fear certainly comes into the picture. For example, it can be scary for women to go out there and make it in the world of work. And it can be scary for men to lose their financial advantage. One man spoke for many when he suggested he was frightened that his wife would no longer want to be with him if he didn't take care of her financially. And, unfortunately, he might be right or, hopefully, he may be wrong.

Remember that even if you have a great relationship, challenges in adjusting to our new freedoms are present in varying degrees for all of us. Let me point out a few of these challenges. As you read, notice where you can see similarities within your own relationship. It is important to bring into consciousness all the subtle and not-so-subtle forces that get in the way of love so that we can do something about them.

Challenge #1
OLD EXPECTATIONS GET
ALL MIXED UP WITH NEW FREEDOMS

Yes, the new freedom in our roles makes for unlimited possibilities. It opens up exciting opportunities for all of us. We are no longer robots falling into the slots that society has created for us. At the same time, since we are still in the process of change, it can also lead to great confusion, resentment and upset. It looks like this:

Woman: "I believe in equality." "What do you mean you want me to pay half the rent?"

Man: "I believe in equality." "What do you mean you want me to help you clean the house?"

Most of our mixed feelings are a lot subtler than that, but the mixed feelings are definitely there. In many ways, we seem to be in a time warp. We say we want the new, but we are consciously or unconsciously upset when we don't get the old. The bottom line is that while both men and women are beginning to see the advantages of equality between the sexes, old stereotypes hang in there and mess with our minds. This inconsistency in our thinking translates into much of the confusion and anger that occurs in our present-day relationships.

Part of the difficulty in accepting the new is that the old sometimes feels very good. On some level, many, if not most, women still love the feeling of being protected. In some holdover from the past, it defines their femininity. Many men still love the role of protector; it defines their masculinity. This is also a holdover from the past. Even very young men and women today have old-time expectations that don't quite fit into today's world where equality is the stated goal. Again, this is totally understandable. Not enough time has passed for the new to become comfortable, logical and actually *much safer for both men and women.*

A case in point: I was invited to be an expert on a television show featuring married couples who were having relationship problems. One of the wives' complaints was, "He doesn't give me enough money." I was a bit surprised. I wouldn't have been so surprised if the show featured a teenager complaining about her father. But, in today's world, something was wrong with the picture of a wife complaining that her husband wouldn't give her enough money, especially since the couple had no children. My question to her was, "Why don't you find a way of earning some money on your own? You're a big girl now!" The audience applauded, as did her husband!

I realize that there are times when it is totally appropriate for one of us to financially support or be supported by the other. But in this particular case, it was the wife's unwillingness to get a job and her inappropriate expectations that were causing her complaints. It was clear that her demands were both childlike and unreasonable—a relic from the past. Not a pretty picture in the present-day world. What she didn't realize was that her safety, her fulfillment, her peace of mind relied on her own ability to take care of herself financially.

There is no question that we have to change our habitual ways of thinking about our roles in relationships. And, of course, the way we do this is to keep our trusty mirror on hand. When we are feeling upset about something our mate is doing or not doing, we have to pick up our mirror and ask ourselves if our upset is legitimate, which sometimes it is, or if it is because of an old and inappropriate expectation.

One of my students, Caroline, was pleased to report that she is picking up her mirror all the time with great results:

"Every time I feel the least bit of resentment arising toward my husband Kenny, I immediately pick up the mirror and ask myself, 'What old expectation is interfering with my loving feelings?' I always come up with an answer. For example, when I'm feeling anxious in any way about my career, my mind reverts to the old stereotype of 'the little woman' being taken care of. When I pick up the mirror it tells me that Kenny and I are in this relationship to take care of each other. I say, 'Grow up, Caroline!' And I remind myself how wonderful it is that I have become as strong and whole as I have become. Taking care of each other is really what it's all about."

I know some of you women out there—and even some men—are asking, "Can we never fall back into the feeling of being taken care of?" Yes, there are times when both men and women can fall into the arms of their mate—when sadness, illness, problems or any difficulties in life happen. We all need a warm, soft place to fall. But we "fall" with the understanding that at the end of the day, we have to pick ourselves up once again. For Mark and me, it is our ability to flow between various roles when appropriate that helps to keep our love alive. Love on a shifting carpet, to be sure. As I see it, *taking care of each other is the most beautiful, satisfying, safe, loving and joyful way of being in a relationship.* This ability to flow in a relationship as situations and needs change is an amazing source of peace of mind.

It is important to remember that, once again, it is usually our fear that keeps us locked in many of our beliefs, actions and expectations. For example, many women have to let go of expectations about money, an area where they are very insecure. Using myself as an example, Mark and I began living together when I was ready to change careers from director of a health facility to author. After leaving my job, it took a few years for me to earn any money; no publisher wanted to buy my first book, *Feel the Fear and Do It Anyway!* (But thankfully, I was persistent!)

When the book was finally published and I began earning money, I noticed my selfish old patterns from my first marriage emerging, with my mind playing with the idea of banking my money and letting Mark continue to support me. Thankfully, I picked up my trusty mirror, which told me, "If that's equality, I'll eat my hat!" So rather than eating my hat, I reluctantly pushed through my resistance and began to contribute my fair share. It was hard in the beginning, but soon it felt great. And now it feels wonderful! I learned that improving my relationship with money definitely improved my ability to feel equal, which is a great feeling indeed. It also increased my ability to love.

Many men are very insecure about their mates growing, stretching and succeeding. They are frightened they won't be needed any more. As their mates get stronger, they feel weaker. I remember a middle-aged man who was constantly belittling his wife and her abilities as she tried to expand her business. When I asked him to pick up the mirror and see what was behind his hurtful behavior, he saw that it was his fear of losing her if she became too successful. He felt very remorseful when he realized that it was his fear that was running him—and hurting her—rather than something based on reality. He apologized and immediately began working on his own insecurities. In a relatively short time, he became a big support to his wife. You can see how the consciousness that comes from looking in the mirror is so important in creating lasting love.

There is an irony here: When we push through our fear, we find a *real* safety that comes from finding our own power. This sense of real safety enhances our ability to be compassionate and caring. As a result, we are able to be much more flexible and loving in our relationships.

Even though some confusion still exists, few of us would want to go back to the way it was. The unhappiness that was lying heavily inside the hearts of so many unfulfilled men and women prior to the new push for equality between the sexes was totally unacceptable. Today a multitude of new choices exists for all of us.

Yes, there are still women who *prefer* to stay at home, look after the kids and tend to hearth and home. And there are still men who *prefer* going off every morning to provide financially for their family. But the difference is that today, IT'S A CHOICE. Happily a wide variety of other choices are available for those who prefer different arrangements. I think that in terms of our options today, it is the best of all possible worlds—even though we still have a way to go.

In today's world, there is no right or wrong role for men and women to play in a relationship. What is important is for us to pick up the mirror, see what would fulfill our purpose in this world and GO FOR IT! Ideally, we are with mates who support what makes us feel fulfilled. Trouble brews when our mate doesn't want to go along with our program. Or when we don't want to go along with theirs. If either is the case, we have to pick up our mirror and get very creative as to how to handle the situation.

I might add that too many of us are still finding ourselves attracted to the "old style" of mate. We have not yet adjusted our eye (and hearts) to the "new style," those who are true friends and partners. This explains why many of us end up disappointed and divorced. Hopefully, we choose better the second time around. Some of us do; some of us don't.

There is no question that letting go of our expectations is a difficult thing to do. Yet, it is our expectations that keep us locked in unhappiness. When we let go of our expectations, we are free to look within, to get in touch with our own power and to derive a new kind of safety that comes from the best of who we are.

Given all that I have said, there is one very powerful, no-lose expectation that I presented in *Opening Our Hearts to Men.* Whether you are a man or woman, I suggest you memorize it and use it to guide you through any difficulties you encounter within your relationship. And that is:

My only expectation of this relationship—whether it lasts one week, twenty-five years, or till death do us part—is that I will learn more about opening my heart and becoming a more loving person. I accept this as one of my highest purposes in life.[2]

Yes, your Higher Purpose rules! As we keep our focus on becoming a more loving person, the improvement in our relationships—and in our lives—can be quite dramatic.

Challenge #2
"OVER-SWINGS" ARE COMMON

In our prior lopsided society, traits such as softness, warmth, emotion and the ability to nurture were assigned to women; and qualities such as strength, assertiveness, rationality and protectiveness were assigned to men. If the truth be known, "masculine qualities" and "feminine qualities" describe qualities that we ALL possess—men and women alike. Men have within them the ability to be soft, warm, nurturing and emotional. Women have within them the ability to be strong, assertive, rational and protective. What I am saying is that:

ALL THESE QUALITIES ARE HUMAN QUALITIES.
THEY ARE NOT EXCLUSIVELY MALE OR FEMALE!

Unfortunately, society has misunderstood this important reality. As a result, most of us were, subtly or not so subtly, trained to be half of what we really are. Women were trained to be soft, warm, nurturing and emotional. Men were trained to be strong, assertive, rational and protective. In recent years we have all, in our own way, been searching for the other half of who we are. The problem is that, in the process, many of us traded one half of ourselves for the other. *The pendulum swung too far.* It looks like this:

Instead of adding the *strong-assertive-rational-protective* to the *soft-warm-nurturing-emotional,* many women simply left the *soft-warm-nurturing-emotional* behind.

Instead of adding the *soft-warm-nurturing-emotional* to *the strong-assertive-rational-protective,* many men left *the strong-assertive-rational-protective* behind.

As a result, too many of us remain lopsided! It is essential that we reclaim what we have lost without losing the strengths we have already gained!

Maybe this over-swing is necessary in the beginning. Maybe some women have to move away from traditional female-ness in order to "own" their sense of power. Maybe some men have to initially move away from traditional male-ness in order to "own" their softer side. One of my students joked that she over-swung into the realm of obnoxious when she began her move into the powerful part of who she was! She said it truly was her own bad behavior that ultimately was one of the major factors in her divorce from her first husband. We could all help the process of inevitable change by picking up the mirror and noticing where we have swung much too far in our efforts to become whole human beings.

The good news is that in time, as we feel more comfortable in our new roles, we are finally able to swing into a more balanced state of mind that represents the totality of ALL of who we are:

soft AND strong AND warm AND assertive AND
nurturing AND rational AND protective AND emotional

Now that's a complete human being! Glorious! And it is beautiful watching both sexes learn how to integrate into their actions and behavior the totality of who they are. It is a new definition of wholeness, and it feels wonderful. Over the years, I have learned to own the male and female within me, and it has made all the difference in the quality of (and equality in) my present marriage.

Wholeness certainly is an important goal and worth all the effort it takes to get you there. You can see how our distorted expectations in a relationship come from a lopsided view of our gender. There is no question in my mind that an ideal relationship is one that comprises two people who have developed the breadth of their talents and emotions. Such a person is rich, vibrant and a true joy to be with. They feel more complete, and their unrealistic expectations of their mate diminish greatly as they understand that they are in control of their own experience of life. This is powerful.

You can also see how feeling complete within ourselves allows us to drop our neediness, which, as you have already learned, is a great destroyer of relationships. The beauty is that *as we feel powerful and whole, we are able to help our mate feel powerful and whole as well* ... a key element in a loving relationship.

Challenge #3
EXPERTS HAVE CONFLICTING OPINIONS

Many would disagree with the idea that men and women are emotionally similar as I describe above. It is true that, on many levels, men and women still feel and behave very differently. The question is, "Is it nature or nurture?" Certain experts try to explain it in terms of nature: We are biologically different. Other experts try to explain it in terms of nurture: We are trained differently.

Probably it's a little of both, but for the most part, I agree with the latter. While, of course, there are biological differences between the sexes (thank goodness!), I think that in the matter of emotional differences, much of it is about training. Boys cry and are still told, "Boys don't cry." Girls climb trees, and are still told, "Girls don't climb trees." Boys want to play with their sisters' dolls but little trucks are still placed in their hands instead. And so it goes. Our training definitely explains many of the differences in the thoughts and behavior of men and women today.

The reason I feel so many of the differences between men and women are a result of nurture (training) is that I have witnessed these differences disappearing as men and women expand into new roles. For example, more and more men are becoming nurturers as they choose to stay home and take care of the children ... while their wives are becoming providers as they choose to become the primary bread-winners. This represents a total reversal of traditional roles. Society may still look down upon these people for their choices—after all, we are still in a time of transition—but the fact that today we can defy tradition and create our own rules tells us that in terms of innate differences between the sexes, many of the experts have been wrong—and continue to be wrong.

I was dismayed recently to hear a very popular male psychologist tell women, "Women, get over it. This is how we (men) are. Silent, moody, sloppy." I thought to myself, "I wonder what other lies he tells himself to justify his dismal behavior." I certainly felt sorry for his wife! I might add that neither my ex-husband nor my present husband is silent, moody or sloppy! So much for believing all the experts.

One of my students, Lilly, told the class that when she was in the middle of her divorce, she told her therapist (a woman) that she was tempted to give custody of the children to her husband since he was so great with them. Her therapist told her that it is impossible for men to be nurturers, that they simply don't have the same feelings of closeness to their children as women do. Bottom line: It would be wrong to give her husband custody of the children. This didn't sound quite right to Lilly. The therapist didn't really know her husband, but she did. She gave custody of the children to her husband in the divorce, and it is working out beautifully for all concerned. Happily, for both men and women, more and more couples are following Lilly's lead.

Similarly, for many years, certain experts have told us that it is biologically determined that women are "nesters" while men like to roam. Yet I recently read an article in the *Sunday Times* about a study showing that the tables have turned. Single men are more likely than women to want to settle down and marry.[3] According to the article, women have become more confident and adventurous, and men have become more insecure and anxious. Furthermore, men want someone to rely on. Richard Scase, professor of sociology at Kent University, is quoted in the article as saying, "We now have more assertive, self-confident women, who are much more aspirational than men, more risk-taking and more enterprising." While I'm skeptical of most studies out there, I would suspect that many turn arounds in the behavior of men and women have occurred as we have become freer to expand our roles.

The point is, don't let the opinions of experts (including me) affect your choice of how to be in a relationship. Maybe they're right; maybe they're wrong. You have to rely on your own wisdom by picking up the mirror, looking inside, seeing what feels right for you and then following your heart.

Challenge #4
OLD TRADITIONS CONFUSE
THE ISSUE OF EQUALITY

So many long-held traditions, which on the surface seem very innocent and sometimes very beautiful, still hold. For example, fathers continue to "give" the bride away to another man who will take care of her. Whoops! Not a symbol of equality between a man and woman. When I married Mark, we walked down the aisle holding hands, symbolic of our walking through life together. My daughter, Leslie, had both my ex-husband and me walk her down the aisle. She chose to think of it as her parents symbolically walking her to a brand-new adult life with her husband, Michael. If you want your father to walk you down the aisle, beautiful—I don't want to break any father's hearts—but it is critical to keep this thought foremost in your mind:

> "I love my father. I know this will make him happy. I am thrilled he is here to walk me down the aisle. I also have to remember that I am an adult who can now take care of myself, and where necessary, take care of my husband as well. Thanks goodness we can take care of each other. Hallelujah!"

193

And men, as your bride is being walked down the aisle with her father, you have to keep in mind:

"While her father is walking her down the aisle and 'giving' her away, she is not my child to take care of; she is my wife. We will walk down the aisle of life together as equals, taking care of each other. Hallelujah!"

Beautiful thoughts for men and women to embrace.

Another very seductive tradition is that of a woman taking her husband's name. To many it implies a woman being under the protective umbrella of her husband. You may have noticed that Mark and I have different last names. In my first marriage, I took my husband's name. When I divorced, I didn't want my ex-husband's name, nor did I want to go back to my father's name. I wanted a new name for a new life. My mother loved the idea. So, after coming up with many names together, we picked the name "Jeffers." It just felt right. When I married Mark, I knew I would not change my name to his. And happily, he never expected me to. Symbolically, my new name reminded me that I was my own person. I didn't belong to anyone else. I suppose I needed that reminder. Understand that I have no problem if you want to, or already have, changed your name to that of your husband's. Just keep reminding yourself of your wholeness and your ability to stand on your own two feet as an equal partner in love.

Interestingly, and surprisingly, Anthony, my step-daughter Alice's husband, took HER name! This was because Alice did not want to change her name and he wanted them to have the same last name. No problem; He would simply change his name to hers. This is the first example I have seen of a man taking his wife's name—and, hopefully, it won't be the last.

Again, on the surface, the lovely traditions of an earlier era are harmless. But in terms of changing our deepest assumptions about who we are, they slow down the process. Of course, don't denigrate yourself for following certain rituals. Just keep in mind what they stand for and remember how important it is for you and your partner to come together as equals in your relationship so that you can help each other live a loving, productive and meaningful life.

Challenge #5
SCORE CARDS ABOUND

Another problem that comes up in today's new world of freedom has to do with partnership. In a loving relationship, we are not keeping score to see who does more or who does less. "I did this for you; now you have to do that for me." Ideally, partners work for the good of all concerned. We do what needs to be done without the pettiness that keeping score implies. We move together and fill our love life with a sense of harmony and flow. Partnership doesn't work if it's a contest to see who does more and who does less.

Of course, there are times when we all feel overburdened in our relationships. We may be feeling tired and/or resentful. If this is true for you, here's a good strategy to try:

1) To soften any anger and resentment you may have, look at the gifts your mate brings to your life. Appreciation of the good always helps us balance out the bad.

2) Pick up the mirror and notice where you are feeling overburdened.

3) With appreciation in mind, work out some possible changes in your lifestyle that would relieve your sense of being overburdened.

4) When you are clear, very clear, within your own mind, lovingly discuss these ideas with your mate. It sounds something like this:

> "Honey, I'm having some problems here. How can we fix it so that it works for both of us?"

You'll note that blame is out of the picture. This approach may or may not work, depending on your particular situation, but there is no question that a loving and clear approach to the problem stands the best chance of attaining a win-win solution for both of you.

Ideally, partners work together to create the rules of the partnership. Every couple is different, and the rules that are good for one couple are not necessarily good for another. Obviously, any rules we create are not etched in stone. As times or situations change, the rules can be altered. But even if your mate is unwilling to work with you, your mirror is your greatest tool. It can tell you what you need to do to make the situation work for you—one way or another.

Challenge #6
TIMES CHANGE; WE CHANGE

Even if we have enjoyed compatibility of roles for a number of years, one of us may change our mind as to how we want to live our life. For example, for many years, Cathleen was totally happy as a wife and mother. At some point, she decided she wanted to go back to college and complete her degree. The carpet truly shifted in her relationship with her husband. Because he was strong enough to support her desire to go back to college, the shifting carpet caused few problems. Of course, in the beginning some practical difficulties had to be ironed out, but it didn't take long for the new patterns of life to work beautifully.

Bill, on the other hand wanted to become a writer after years of working very hard in a career he didn't enjoy. While he and his wife would have to cut back a bit financially, her salary could easily cover their living expenses. Unfortunately, his wife wouldn't go along with the plan. Resentment slowly built up in Bill as a result of feeling trapped in a life he no longer chose to live. Not a good scenario.

In an ideal relationship, we don't get hung up on roles. We are both strong enough to roll with the changes. The key is not to become too rigid in our positions and to learn the meaning of flow. A big challenge indeed! Even those who are adept at flowing with the changes in life often have an initial reaction of fear as changes occur. With the proper tools, such as those I present in this book and my other books, we can push past the fear and once again roll with the changes.

Again, there is no right or wrong way to be in a relationship. We have to create our own rules as we go along. It is the "process" of relationship that is so important—and challenging. Do we use the relationship to learn how to become a more loving person, or do we continue to be stuck in making demands of our partner based on our own insecurities?

There is no question that as our relationship moves forward, we are frequently caught in the middle of discovery and confusion. As I see it, no matter what happens in a relationship, it is all an opportunity to learn more about who we are, what we still have to learn and what we have to be grateful for.

For the first time in recent history, every couple is on their own to discover how to build a healthy relationship and to forge their own vision of how and why to be together. It is a time of big challenges—wonderful challenges! We need to create a deep awareness—a deep consciousness—as to where we are still stuck. And, of course, the greatest tool is our mirror.

Challenge #7
WE HAVE TO CREATE NEW REASONS
FOR RELATIONSHIPS

There is no question that many of the old reasons for being in a relationship are gone. As men learn how to cook, clean and care for children, they don't need anyone to do it for them. As women learn how to take care of themselves financially, they don't need anyone to earn money for them. I actually heard a woman say, "Who needs men at all? I can raise my kids, earn my own money and be free of men." I thought to myself, "Poor woman! She doesn't have a clue as to how wonderful it is to truly love and be loved by a beautiful human being with whom she can share her life."

Today relationships are not founded on dependency as they once were. People have more choice about who to be with and who not to be with—or whether to be with anyone at all. Personally, I consider this VERY GOOD NEWS. We now have an opportunity to be in a relationship for much more fulfilling reasons than in earlier times. It's no longer about survival; *it's about learning and growing together; it's about supporting each other's dreams; it's about the wonder of walking the walk and talking the talk.* These are beautiful components of real love, in which men and women help each other to become whole. It is a life long process and it is wonderful to *grow* old together.

As I look around, I see many signs that both men and women alike are beginning to see advantages in their expanded roles:

- More and more women are enjoying work, while men are enjoying more involvement with their families.

- More and more women are feeling more powerful as they develop their talents, while men are feeling less pressure to provide all the income.

- More and more women are feeling more secure knowing they can provide income for the family instead of always being a dependent, while more and more men are proud of the professional accomplishments of their wives.

- More and more men are turned on by strong women, while more and more women are turned on by warm and caring men.

- More and more men and women are looking to find a true partner in love—to share, to enjoy, to take care of each other.

I thought you would enjoy the following encouraging comments from some of the men and women I have interviewed:

"I've been trained to be in control. But I think that love is more important than control. And certainly more powerful!"

"There is no question that my wife is my equal. I love it. Why would I want to be married to someone who is less than I am?"

"Yes, I get confused sometimes, but I certainly wouldn't want to go back to the way it was. My husband and I are, little by little, learning to be ourselves and supporting each other in being ourselves."

"I love getting in touch with my so-called feminine side. When I make a delicious dinner for my wife, when I bathe my son and put him to bed, when I help my wife keep our house in order, I love it! To be able to be a part of it all is wonderful!"

"I feel so safe in my relationship since I feel I can be who I want to be without criticism from my husband. It makes me appreciate how lucky I am."

"I really don't want to be the caretaker of my wife. It's like carrying around extra baggage. It's difficult enough for us to take care of the kids. And why should I take care of my wife? She's old enough and smart enough to take care of herself."

"For the first time, I am getting a sense of what love feels like. We validate each other. We appreciate each other. Any anger is quickly dispelled. I was a little nervous about her independence in the beginning, but now I see the advantages. I used to get something from being the strong one in control, but I realize I lost a lot as well. I feel much more myself in this relationship. I am able to express my feelings; we both can. The threat is gone. It feels terrific."

"I think that we are all confused. It's a search for all of us. My husband struggles with it just as I do. But as we walk the path together, I feel a deep sense of happiness that we are together. Yes, at times our insecurities will take over and cause some problems, but as we explore them together, we will come out of it okay, as we always have in the past."

We're not there 100 percent. Total acceptance of the freedom we now have will take a while, but I do believe a day will come when women will say, "Could you believe we expected men to do this for us?" And men will say, "Could you believe we expected women to do this for us?" Both will say, "What were we thinking?"

When I presented these concepts in one of my workshops, I expected a lot of resistance, but instead I saw a lot of relief on the faces of everyone sitting before me. It's as though they had been given an explanation, an answer, a pathway to follow. Some of the confusion as to why love was so hard had been dispelled. Some of the attendees cried softly. It was a very moving moment.

Women can't go back to being the children they were in those "good" old days and men can't go back to being the "daddies" they were to their wives. No, we need to walk the walk together, side by side, each contributing to the grandeur of an adult "stirring the oatmeal" kind of relationship together. How beautiful this is!

LOVE LESSONS

1) ***Analyze your expectations.*** In no other area do we need to pick up the mirror more than we do relative to our old expectations and new freedoms. Take some time to write down the answers to the following questions:

- What do I really expect from my mate?

- Where am I stuck in old ways of thinking about how a relationship should be?

- How do I remain whole without losing myself to my mate?

- How do I maintain my lovingness while fulfilling my own dreams?

- Where are my expectations inconsistent with my stated desires?

Women, you also need to ask yourselves questions such as:

"Why do I expect him to be financially responsible, yet criticize him when he works long hours and doesn't spend enough time with the family?"

Men, you also need to ask yourselves questions such as:

"Why do I expect my wife to take so much responsibility for the children and the house when we both are working?"

Really analyzing our inconsistencies and expectations requires consciousness. We have to be aware as to where old habits of thinking are getting in the way of a loving relationship. Without consciousness we just keep doing the same relationship-defeating actions over and over again. And a break-up is often inevitable. It is important to look inside to see what we can do to become more loving people, which, as you have already learned, is the most important purpose of our relationship.

2) *Teach each other.* Men and women have much to learn from one another, but we have to be willing to learn. There are so many things that women can't do because they weren't taught. There are so many things that men can't do because they weren't taught. So let's begin a new kind of education in which, in our effort to become whole and equal partners, we can learn from one another. For example, if they don't already know how:

- Men, teach the women how to change a tire; and, women, be willing to learn.

- Women, teach the men how to prepare dinner, and, men, be willing to learn.

- Men, teach women all you know about managing money, and, women, be willing to learn.

- Women, do all the driving for a while, until it feels natural not to have your man drive, and, men, let them.

You get the picture. Think of all the stereotypical ways of being in a relationship and change the picture. Many of you have already learned so much from members of the opposite sex, and I'm sure you will agree that the more we know, the more complete we feel as human beings. So make learning and teaching an enriching part of your relationships with members of the opposite sex.

3) ***Put your anger to good use.*** Anger is a good clue that our expectations are in control and they are getting in the way of love. If we use our inappropriate anger to hurt our mate, our relationship is in danger. On the other hand, if we use our inappropriate anger as a vehicle for growth, then it is a valuable emotion. How do we do that? It's easy. We pick up the mirror and once again ask ourselves such important questions as, "What am I not doing for myself that I am expecting him/her to do for me?" "How can I change what isn't working?" Remember:

**When we begin taking responsibility for
our experience of life, our anger disappears.**

Anger feels powerful, but unless it is used to teach us what we need to work on within ourselves, it is actually powerless. It fools us into thinking we are correct in all our unloving thoughts. It is also an important clue that we are not in control of our reactions. It causes us to blame our mates. It says we are victims. And unless we pick up the mirror, our anger can become vicious and ugly. Just witness many divorce proceedings.

You can understand why the mirror is so important when we are feeling angry. When we take responsibility for our own lives, our anger disappears and we stop blaming our mate. Powerful indeed!

I put only love into this world I put only love

Chapter 13

WE OWE TO OURSELVES ...
WE OWE IT TO EACH OTHER

If you live your life on the basis of a trashy novel,
the Universe will follow suit. But if you live your
life as a cosmic identity, like someone who matters,
then the Universe will take you seriously!
—MARIANNE WILLIAMSON[1]

I want to end this section of the book by talking about a very broad problem that looms large and affects too many relationships today, often without our realizing it. I speak of the so-called "war between the sexes." You might be wondering what the war between the sexes could possibly have to do with your ability to create a lasting love. It's as simple as this:

If you don't love, respect and admire the opposite sex, you won't, by definition, love, respect and admire your mate.*

---

*This, of course, does not apply to homosexual relationships ... or does it? If we have unresolved conflict with any members of the human race, we have much to work on relative to our being free to love in a relationship.

It makes sense, doesn't it? I strongly believe that your general feelings about the opposite sex set the tone for your personal relationships. And even if you love the opposite sex, please read this chapter. You can play an important part in ending this destructive war.

Let me begin with a little history. Some erroneously believe that the war between the sexes began with the woman's movement in the 1960's. You may be shocked to learn that way back in 1897, a woman from Queensland was angry enough to distribute to as many women as she possibly could an eight-stage *detailed* recipe for cooking a husband![2] I think it's a safe bet that this woman never did create a beautiful love with her husband—or any other man. Unfortunately, after all these years, not much has changed. In the late 1980s, a women's conference in Ottawa, Canada was selling a badge with the words, "The only good man is a dead one." In 2002, writer Keira Wagner tells us that some radical feminists are still preaching the same ugly message.[3]

Of course, women don't wage this war alone; men have their own armaments as well. Actually you can find website after website filled with male-bashing and female-bashing jokes. I understand they are only joking … maybe. But we're talking here about creating a beautiful love. And I'm just pointing out that these kinds of jokes just don't contribute to the cause.

Yes, the war between the sexes thrives even now in the 21st century. Actually it's big, very big! And, if we are in an unconscious mode, we may not even notice that this destructive war is causing such unhappiness, or that it's even raging, or that it's often very hurtful. In fact, we unwittingly may be encouraging it. For example, we may laugh when a joke is told about members of the opposite sex—often when our mates are in the room. We all love a good laugh, but do we want to laugh when someone else is being put down?

There is no question that we need to become more aware and stop treating members of the opposite sex with such disregard.

This means:

- We notice that what is absent in the put-downs of the opposite sex is a sense of caring and compassion.

- We notice how unloving it is to build ourselves up at the expense of others whom we are putting down.

- We notice how we are hurting other people by our insensitivity.

- We notice that there is an ugliness about making fun of other people.

I ask you, *don't you wonder why many more of us are not offended by all this gender-bashing?* I truly believe that part of the reason is that we often are not aware of the damage we are doing to others, including our own mate. And what about ourselves? Whether we are aware of it or not, such behavior eats away at our self-esteem.

Ironically, most of us pride ourselves on being loving and caring people. Yet when we participate in the bashing of members of the opposite sex, we are behaving in a hurtful and unloving way. On the other hand, by acting in a way that respects and honors members of the opposite sex, we form the basis of a new kind of relationship with ourselves and others: one of compassion, caring and love. And:

**The love of the opposite sex definitely
translates into love for our mate.**

Yes, for many, many reasons, it's time to end this soul-destroying war and create a sense of peaceful and joyful mutual love between men and women. "Why would anyone resist?" is the big question. But resist we do. I remember when *Opening Our Hearts to Men* was published, I appeared on a television show with a very hostile female presenter. She began the interview with, "I bet the feminists must hate you, writing a book with this title!" Since I thought the title was very loving and hopeful, I was taken aback, to say the least. I responded with:

"Excuse me! I am a feminist. But I didn't know the women's movement was about hating men. I thought it was about women becoming the best that they could be, and certainly women hating men is not the best they can be! I'm proud to be a woman who loves men!"

I was on a roll. I was on my soapbox. Nothing could stop me now. I went on to explain:

"I learned to love men by doing what all women, whether they consider themselves feminists or not, need to be doing: standing tall, taking responsibility for their experiences in life, spreading their love into this world. And that includes their love of men. Furthermore, liberation is about letting our light shine through. It has nothing to do with men! It's about becoming the best that we can be. It's about pulling out of ourselves all the power and love we can muster. It's about walking around feeling great about ourselves for all the love and caring we are putting into this world, not about how much hate we are putting into this world. It's about taking charge of our lives, honoring who we are. When we do, our anger disappears. And what is there to be angry about when we take responsibility for our experiences in life? Nothing."

The presenter tried very hard to negate everything I was saying and, in the end, her animosity was a clear demonstration of all the points I was trying to make.

And then there were the book signings. While most of the women applauded me for writing such a book, there were also some who angrily confronted me with: "Open our hearts to *them?* No way! Why don't they open their hearts to *us?*" I then explained that, of course, men need to open their hearts as well, but because *Opening Our Hearts to Men* was written to empower women, men's issues were not the focus of the book.

For many years after the breakup of my first marriage, I admit that I was a champion male-basher: "Would you believe he did this? Would you believe he did that?" And all my wonderful "moan and groan" female buddies nodded in disbelief and shared their "Would you believe ... ?" stories. We were so self-righteously convinced we were the superior of the species. "If only we could find a man with the superior qualities of our female friends." And in the middle of it all, *I couldn't understand why I couldn't find a man who was kind and loving.* A look in the mirror would have explained a lot!

Thankfully, I ultimately learned the error of my ways, which allowed me to create a blessedly satisfying relationship—which is what I wish for all who are reading this book. Yes, I have learned that both men and women need to drop their swords and become partners in this wonderful, but sometimes difficult, journey through life. Here are just a few of the 101 reasons I came up with as to why we should do this:

- *It's time!* I'm sure you'll agree that the war between the sexes has gone on much too long. There are some who actually love war; it gives them a reason to be. Sad, but true. On the other hand, for most of us, war is heavy, hurtful and takes away the true joy in life ... and love. For many reasons, it's time to end this soul-destroying war and create a sense of peaceful and joyful co-existence between men and women. I have taken my own journey from war to peace and from hate to love, and this journey has transformed my entire experience of life and love.

- *There are no winners in the war between the sexes.* It has often been said that the difference between human beings and rats is that both can be trained to go down a path in a maze to find the cheese. If the cheese is taken away, eventually the rats will stop their fruitless search and try another path. Human beings seem to go down the same path over and over again, even if the cheese is no longer there! Crazy, isn't it? One has only to look at the divorce rate and all the other ramifications of the war between the sexes to understand that anger and hate do not work. It's time to look for a path that brings more harmony and love into this world and into our personal lives.

- *Like attracts like.* Let's face it. If you are an angry and bitter person, healthy members of the opposite sex would be smart to turn and run the other way. I'm sure anger and bitterness contribute to the high divorce rate. Warm, soft and loving people want to be around other warm, soft and loving people. It stands to reason that as our hearts open up, our relationships will get better and better. And if we are not in a relationship, we will draw much more loving people into our lives.

- *Love feels better than anger.* Having been a male-basher for many years, I know that anger doesn't feel good. When we act angrily, we become obsessive injustice collectors, never noticing the incredible beauty and abundance that surround us. Now that I have learned how to let go of my anger by dealing with the pain and fear that was lying underneath, life has magically transformed into a heaven on earth. Love is the sublime emotion. Why choose anger when it's possible to choose love? Why break our own hearts?

- *People who love are more attractive than people who hate.* That's a good incentive! And, it's true. With all the advertisements about looking good, the truth is that there is no body-building exercise or face cream that will take away the ugliness of hate and insecurity—both symptoms of a closed heart. So if you are a man or woman concerned about looking your best, it's time to deal with the anger. Sneers and looks of disdain aren't attractive at all. They create a very negative energy that is felt by all who come close, particularly your mate! There is no question in my mind that people who love are more beautiful than people who hate.

- *Warmer beds!* I've been warm and I've been cold. Warm is better. Enemies don't warm beds. When we are angry, we avoid their touch, and we miss the deliciousness of cuddling up and allowing in the warmth of another human being. We miss the beauty of sex between two loving partners. For the emotionally healthy among us, it is hard to see a hateful person as sexy. When we are hateful, we miss so much. Electric blankets are a poor substitute. They simply are not able to say those beautiful words, "I love you." That's just the way it is.

- *Fewer health problems.* There is mounting evidence that anger affects the immune system and opens the doors to such illnesses as cancer and heart disease. Anger feels like a poison in our system. I don't know if anger contributed to the breast cancer I had over twenty years ago, but cancer was definitely my impetus to begin dealing with my anger and learning how to flood my body with love. We worry so much about external pollutants in today's society that we forget about the internal pollutants

213

caused by negativity. Science will prove me right … or wrong, but there is no question that a harmony of body, mind and spirit contributes to a more beautiful experience of life.

• *Frees up so much valuable space in our heads.* When I was in my male-bashing mode, the chatterbox in my mind drove me crazy with its negativity. What a waste of the miracle of the mind! It could have been filled with so many positive things. And then there was the enormous amount of time my friends and I wasted putting down members of the opposite sex. Awful! We could have been talking instead about constructive, life-enhancing opportunities to enrich our lives and the world. It's as though life is on a downward spiral when we are perpetually angry. What takes us off this downward spiral is, again, to deal with the pain and fear that lies behind our upset. It is then that the spiral turns upward once again toward a transcendent and joyful space.

• *Happier children.* We who are parents are so concerned about bringing up healthy and happy children. Yet, when ugly words about members of the opposite sex spew from our mouths, do we think that the children don't notice? When it comes to our children—and our own sense of well-being—we need to be much more responsible for our mouth. And the best way to do this is to let love be the message we give, not anger.

• *Less violence.* The violence between men and women continues. When we harbor hate, we treat people hatefully, and the result is that hate comes back to us. When we love and care for the hearts of others, the violence diminishes. It's as simple as that.

- *Loving members of the opposite sex can make us smarter.* I kid you not. As we put down our swords, we can say to each other, "Teach me about this. Teach me about that." As I pointed out in Chapter 12, what an incredible resource we could be to each other! Our society unwittingly has taught us to be half of what we could be. With greater love between the sexes, we can learn the other half. Men can learn the beauty of nurturing and openness, and women can learn the beauty of assertiveness and power—while still loving the essence of who they are. It is already happening. The good news is that as men and women learn from one another, their level of compatibility can't help but rise to new levels. And our sense of separateness is supplanted by a sense of togetherness. The possibilities are amazing!

- *Love makes life more enjoyable.* Have you ever been out with a warring couple? Have you ever been out with a loving couple? Which is the more enjoyable evening? I personally don't like being in the company of men and women who snipe at each other all the time. My only reaction is, "Get me away from all this negativity!" I'm certain that the warring couple would like to get away from all the negativity as well. Thankfully, they can. All they have to do is become more conscious of what they are doing and begin changing the warring pattern that exists between them.

- *Less infidelity and less divorce.* When we harbor a closed heart, we become hard to live with. Walls around our hearts create intense loneliness—for our mates and for ourselves. We don't allow in the love that can ease our sense of alienation. Not only do we get lonely, but our mates do as well. Also, we don't appreciate the

215

beauty in our mate. Hence one or both of us sometimes strays to find validation in the world outside our marriage. Or we leave. This pattern will repeat itself over and over again, until we learn the lessons of love.

- *Love creates beauty.* The difference in the way the world looks relative to our state of mind is astonishing, and that is understandable. When you see the other half of the human race as beautiful, you see a lot of beauty out there. When you see the other half of the human race as ugly, you see a lot of ugliness out there. Obviously our attitude makes quite a difference in what we see. When our heart opens, beauty washes through us as we look out into the big, wide, wonderful world. We look with eyes of caring, compassion, generosity and all good things. Why choose a closed heart when an open heart makes the world look so much better? And it definitely is a choice.

- *The planet needs our love.* Anger spreads. It's contagious. Happily, as I've already discussed in Chapter 3, love spreads. It's also contagious. And as our hearts become more loving, we add to the critical mass that can transform a world of hate into a world of love. Yes, our love is surely needed right now. The horror going on all over the world is simply a reflection of the jealousy, greed, vengefulness and inflexibility that comes from closed hearts—ours included.

- *Everyone loves a happy ending!* There is no question that the ending to most of our personal stories will be happy as we increase the love in our hearts. A beautiful love can exist only when we open the door to the beauty that lies within our being—and our partner's being. And when that happens, we truly can live happily ever after.

And now for the big question:

CAN YOU THINK OF JUST ONE REASON NOT TO END THE WAR BETWEEN THE SEXES?

I suspect you can't! So let's look beneath the surface:

I believe that the only reason any one of us is unable to end our own personal war between the sexes is that we are too frightened to look inside, acknowledge where we have failed to take responsibility for our own lives and then take that responsibility.

Please read that last sentence again. Remember that I've been there, done that. And I know that it *seems* much less frightening to remain unconscious and blame the "enemy." But at some point we have to ask ourselves, "Do we really want to live our lives this way?" We have to ask ourselves, "Is this path that we're on leading to better relationships, more fulfilled lives and the joyful embracing of life's experiences?" You and I both know that the answer to each of these questions is "NO." In fact, this negativity is leading us to alienation, loneliness, bitterness, emptiness and a life fraught with unhappy relationships. It's time to push through the fear, pick up our true power and become a caring and loving human being.

It's probably true that the war between the sexes won't end for quite a while. But the good news is that, in order to create a beautiful love, we don't have to be concerned about the big wide world out there. *We only have to take control of our own words, our own actions and our own hearts.* This means that if you are in any way engaged in the war between the sexes, you can learn how to drop your sword, turn around and run in a different direction—toward a more loving and satisfying way of connecting with members of the opposite sex. We constantly need to ask ourselves:

217

- How can we wake up and take notice?

- How can we become conscious enough to stop a habit that is ingrained in our being?

- How can we throw any gender bashing out of our own lives?

- How in our own lives can we stop the war?

Obviously, we need tools and reminders to help us turn our habits of negativity into habits of love. The following Love Lessons contain a few very effective exercises to help you create a win-win situation between you and the man/woman in your life and the men/women in the world.

LOVE LESSONS

1) *Very important: learn the value of the word "some."* "Some" is the word that will help you avoid lumping all men and women together. We often hear people say, "Men. They're all alike." Or "Women. They're all alike." Wrong! Men aren't all alike; nor are women all alike.

It is common, even among professionals who should know better, to generalize when speaking about members of the opposite sex. "Why do men always do this?" "Why do women always do that?" It is very important that we stop generalizing and include the very valuable word "SOME." "Why do *SOME* women do this?" "Why do *SOME* men do this?" Don't you feel an immediate shift in your attitude? We need only to look around to notice that:

SOME men are sloppy; **SOME** women are sloppy.
SOME men are neat; **SOME** women are neat.

SOME men are nurturing; **SOME** women are nurturing.
SOME men are not nurturing; **SOME** women are not nurturing.

SOME men prefer staying at home with the children;
SOME women prefer staying at home with the children.

SOME men prefer the workplace;
SOME women prefer the workplace.

SOME men are rational; **SOME** women are rational.
SOME men are emotional; **SOME** women are emotional.

SOME men are violent; **SOME** women are violent.
SOME men are gentle and loving; **SOME** women are gentle and loving.

I could go on, but you get the picture.

From my own personal experience, I don't understand why these stereotypes exist. For example, I have heard some women saying, "Men are such slobs." As I've already told you, I am a slob and I am definitely a woman, and for some strange reason, both my first husband and my second husband are very neat. For both of their sakes, I have tried, and continue to try, very hard to tidy up after myself out of consideration and embarrassment, but I have to admit, this isn't "natural" for me.

Another example of an erroneous stereotype: On television recently, I was very moved by a story about a soldier. His wife, also a soldier, was called to duty in another part of the world, leaving him to care for their three young children. He was a soldier by day, a father by night. As you saw him interacting with his children, his tenderness and caring came through loud and clear. There was love all around. He said it was insulting to him when people assume that only women can be the caregivers to their children. He says, "I know I can take care of my kids just as well as my wife can." And watching him nurture his children, I'm sure it is true.

As to men not being as emotional as women, again I can't agree. Maybe society has taught men to hide it better, but the emotion is definitely there. Recently, I've been informally counseling a number of men whose wives have left them. Trust me when I tell you that they are more emotional and broken-hearted than some women I have counseled whose husbands have left. Their lives feel empty and, at times, they feel suicidal. Research has show that many more men commit suicide than women when a relationship ends. Yes, some men are deeply emotional.

So from now on: (a) Remember to say "SOME men" and "SOME women" to remind you that they are not all the same, and (b) pay attention to where the stereotypes about men and women, such as those described above, simply don't hold up.

2) *Point out to others what they are doing.* Become conscious of those times when others are putting down members of the oppo-

site sex and lovingly tell them to stop. This allows you to participate in ending the war by helping others to break their bad habit.

For example: You are sitting around with some of your friends and someone, either male or female, makes a gender-bashing joke. Everyone laughs. When this happens, push through the fear of a backlash and say, "Let's stop the female/male bashing here. Let's talk about what we love about men/women." Remind them that fun at the expense of another makes us less than we want to be. I believe that a person on the road to health will thank you for this; as we all know, we don't even notice our habits until someone points them out to us. If they don't thank us, or don't even agree with us, we have to ask ourselves whether we want to hang out with angry, negative people. As you move further on the path toward love, the answer will definitely be, "NO."

3) *Begin to notice the subtle and not-so-subtle gender bashing in our world.* It is everywhere: on television (often on the top comedy shows), in books, in advertisements and so on. You will even find it where it definitely shouldn't be—in the arena of therapy.

One of my students told me that she stopped therapy because her therapist was fuelling the war between the sexes by asserting that women are inherently superior. I don't know where the therapist got her misinformation, but she obviously needs to go back to school. There is no evidence that, generally speaking, either sex is inherently superior to the other. This therapist clearly has issues with the opposite sex and really needs help herself.

Interestingly, as you embark on your own journey to making men and women lovers instead of fighters, you will no longer find any of these put-downs appealing or appropriate. And the more conscious of this issue you become, the more you will notice this negativity ... and the more you will be encouraged to change it in your own life and in your own interaction with others.

Why should any of us—men or women—open our hearts to members of the opposite sex? I'll tell you why. Because opening our hearts is an act of *self*-love. Nothing could be as sad as going though life with a closed heart. Always remember:

When you open your heart, you not only let the love out, you also let it in. Heaven!

4) *Investigate any men's or women's workshops you may be thinking of attending.* The advertisements for men's and women's workshops can be very deceiving. I once saw a workshop advertising that it would help women gain their power. It sounded good. Out of curiosity, I called to get more details. The leader of the workshop answered the phone. I asked her what she was planning to cover. She explained that since women are so oppressed, it is important to deal with the pain and upset that men cause. Oh, my!

I then said the following in a very non-confrontational voice: "You're right that in some areas women have been oppressed. But, in some areas, men have been oppressed as well." As an example I pointed out that I didn't have the psychological burden of supporting a man financially. When my children were growing up, I had the option of going out to work or staying home with my children—whatever I wanted. My ex-husband didn't have that choice; his "role" was to take care of us. I said that, in some ways, both sexes are oppressed, and we have to work together to make true equality possible for all of us. As rationally as I tried to talk with her, this woman became so irate that I wasn't buying into the victim mentality that she hung up on me. *She is leading workshops*!

In any case, investigate first, and if you find yourself in a men's or women's group or workshop where the victim mentality is evident, speak up. Risk being unpopular. Perhaps one person in that room will hear you. Again, the less self-righteous and more loving you are when you speak up, the more likely it is that you will be heard ... maybe.

5) *Look with eyes of compassion at members of the opposite sex.* Always look beneath the surface. No matter how many people try to tell you that women and men come from different planets,

the truth is that, at the end of the day, we are all human beings just doing the best we can at any given moment of our lives. All of us—yes, men and women alike—feel pain relative to certain happenings in our lives; all of us want to love and be loved; all of us want to be successful in our chosen roles, and so on. Of course, our physiology may be different, which is a good thing relative to keeping the human race alive, and we definitely differ in terms of our training. But on an emotional level, most of us want the same things: peace, love, fulfillment and a sense that we matter.

Knowing this, when your partner is watching television or reading a book or is generally preoccupied, I suggest you stop for a moment and take a good "deep" look. See the hopes, the dreams and the fears that lie beneath the surface and let your heart go out to him/her. Say to yourself:

> "This is a person just like me ... who experiences the same difficult emotions that as I do—fear, frustration, anger, all of it—who wants to be loved, just like me. I will do everything I can to make her/his life beautiful."

We are often unconscious as to the feelings of our partner. You now have the opportunity to wake up and feel compassion, one of the most beautiful and loving of human emotions. Lucy, one of my students, tried this exercise as she was watching her husband play with their son. She was astounded at how moved she felt, and she promised herself that she would never look at him in the same judgmental way she had in the past.

If you are not in a relationship, it is important to "embrace" members of the opposite sex. A potential mate would be stupid to look for love among those who are angry, cynical and disdainful. A healthy person will gravitate toward people with open hearts, not those who view them with disdain.

Whether in a relationship or not, begin taking a good "deep" look at all members of the opposite sex. Even if her/his behavior is upsetting, just remember author and motivational speaker Zig

Ziglar's wonderful line, "Every obnoxious act is a cry for help." Let's help each other—not fight each other—as we travel this sometimes very difficult road together.

6) *Apologize.* In one of her workshops, Marianne Williamson instructed the men and women in attendance to stand face to face and offer each other this very dramatic and beautiful apology:

"If I, or any member of my sex, has ever done anything to hurt you, please forgive me … and please forgive us."[4]

Say these words to yourself right now. Do you feel your heart melt? Can you imagine how things might change if you and your mate faced each other and said these moving words? Mark and I stood before each other and said these beautiful words to each other, and we were moved to tears.

Can you imagine what the world would look like if all men and all women could face each other and say these moving words? What a wonderful way to end the war between the sexes and begin our collective journey on the pathway to love. While we can't control the rest of the world, I suggest you do this with your mate. Just stand face to face and say these beautiful words to each other.

And don't stop there. When walking down the street, silently repeat these beautiful words to members of the opposite sex who are passing by. Imagine the energy of caring and love you are radiating. It will heal your heart, and begin to heal the hearts of all those to whom you spread your love.

7) *Stop playing the role of the victim.* I've talked throughout this book about the dangers of creating yourself as a victim. Victim-hood is a sad, helpless focus on the self. Men are not victims, women are not victims—unless they choose to be. The other sex didn't do it to us; we allowed it to happen, and we can now make the choice to change it. Remember that when we play the role of the victim, we are giving away all our power. We are not

pushing through the fear and taking action necessary to create what we want in our own lives.

So when you hear yourself blaming the opposite sex, including your mate, for all your problems, pick up the mirror and ask:

"HOW CAN *I* CHANGE WHAT IS NOT WORKING?"

That's a very powerful question. Too many of us just keep pointing the finger and refuse to take responsibility, and we remain a victim of our own making. It doesn't have to be that way. Thankfully, we all can begin our own personal journey of pushing through the fear, moving from a position of pain to one of power and creating a beautiful life.

I understand that making that journey from anger to love isn't the easiest thing to do. Anger feels good sometimes. It has a false sense of power. Also it masks the fear, the sense of threat and the pain that lies beneath. It's definitely time to take off the mask and search for the truth that lies underneath. This search is well worth the effort. Being perpetually angry is most hurtful to ourselves.

Always remember that the underlying reasons for our anger have little to do with the so-called "enemy." In the end, they have to do with our not taking charge of our lives and honoring who we are as human beings. And, as you have already learned, what underlies everything is our fear.

When we do push through our fear, take charge of our lives and honor who we are, let me tell you what happens. Our fear is abated. We lay down our swords. Our warring tendencies disappear. We are at peace. We feel happy within ourselves. We feel in control of our lives. And, as a result, we open our hearts and our arms and allow in the greatest feeling in the world ... LOVE! Fantastic! We owe it to ourselves; we owe it to each other.

225

I commit I commit I commit I commit I commit I
commit I commit I commit I commit I commit I commit
I commit I commit I commit I commit I commit I
commit I commit I commit I commit I commit I commit
I commit I commit I commit I commit I commit
I commit I commit I commit I commit I commit I
I commit I commit I commit I commit I commit I
commit I commit I commit I commit I commit I commit
I commit I commit I commit I commit I commit
I commit I commit I commit I commit I commit
commit I commit I commit I commit I commit I
commit I commit I commit I commit I commit I commit
I commit I commit I commit I commit I commit I
commit I commit I commit I commit I commit I commit
I commit I commit I commit I commit I commit
I commit I commit I commit I commit I commit
commit I commit I commit I commit I commit I
commit I commit I commit I commit I commit I commit
I commit I commit I commit I commit I commit I
commit I commit I commit I commit I commit I commit
I commit I commit I commit I commit I commit
I commit I commit I commit I commit I commit I
commit I commit I commit I commit I commit I
commit I commit I commit I commit I commit I commit
I commit I commit I commit I commit I commit I
commit I commit I commit I commit I commit I commit
I commit I commit I commit I commit I commit
I commit I commit I commit I commit I commit I
commit I commit I commit I commit I commit I commit
I commit I commit I commit I commit I commit

CONCLUSION

GUESS WHAT I FINALLY FOUND!

Don't walk behind me, I may not lead.
Don't walk in front of me, I may not follow.
Just walk beside me and be my friend.
　　　　　　　　　　　　　—ALBERT CAMUS

I had to come very far on my journey through life before I finally found what so many of us say we are looking for. Have you guessed what I finally found? I won't keep you in suspense a moment longer. What I finally found was ... my Soul Mate! Where did I find him? It's hard to believe. I was eating dinner with my wonderful husband of many years. I turned to look at him and, in a shock of heavenly recognition, there he was! Right before my eyes! Sitting beside me!

Before that moment of recognition, I believed that finding a Soul Mate was one of those overblown idealizations of love that really wasn't attainable. I once heard a spiritual teacher joke that the likelihood of finding your Soul Mate was very remote. She suggested that we should console ourselves with the fact that we are with someone else's. While I still laugh at her joke, I have

227

finally realized that she was wrong, at least in my case. The big discovery for me was that:

**YOU "FIND" YOUR SOUL MATE OVER TIME IN
THE PROCESS OF LIVING AND LOVING TOGETHER.**

It doesn't happen all at once as we have been led to believe. It takes a while for true Soul Mate status to be conferred. Before the beautiful bond between two souls can be created:

• You have to go through the difficult times.

• You have to appreciate the wonderful times.

• You have to work through the petty differences.

• You have to learn to communicate with love.

• You have to push through the fear and grow into a strong, loving and caring person.

• You have to lighten up and laugh at your humanness.

It stands to reason, therefore, that your Soul Mate is *not* that person you instantly fall in love with across the proverbial crowded room. Over time, he/she may ultimately become your Soul Mate. But it takes time ... and loving ... and caring ... and appreciating. Usually when I interview happy long-married couples, I hear a version of, "We are more in love today than we were in the beginning." Yes, Soul Mate status assures more happiness today than we had in the beginning—in fact, much more happiness in the relationship than we ever could have imagined.

And once that beautiful bond is created, you develop a "knowing" as to what pleases the other. You develop a desire to protect each other, to touch each other, to be together and to share together. It's a very blissful feeling indeed. Mark and I have been together for over twenty-two years (married nineteen) and, more than ever, my heart sings when he walks in the door. He brings me pleasure, as I try to bring pleasure to him.

This leads me to something else I discovered:

**YOU WILL NEVER GET TO SOUL MATE STATUS
UNLESS YOU LIVE PRIMARILY
IN THE REALM OF YOUR SOUL!***

This means that if you want to "find" your Soul Mate, you have to become someone who lives in your soul, what I love to call the Higher Self. As I explained earlier, the Higher Self is that loving, caring, joyful, appreciative, respectful, kind and giving part of us. The more time we are able to spend in the soul-part of who we are, the more we are able to transform the unloving to the loving. We could call this "Soul Mate training."

Putting soul into everything we do requires that we honor our commitments. In terms of our relationships, what does commitment really mean? As I see it, a commitment is a personal pledge to contribute to the happiness and well-being of our mate. Here are a few commitments required for an eventual Soul Mate connection:

- *I commit* to working on the fears that get in the way of my ability to love.
- *I commit* to saying loving things to my mate.
- *I commit* to saying loving things about my mate.
- *I commit* to making his/her life easier.
- *I commit* to appreciating all the good he/she puts into my life.

---

*Note: If you are not in a relationship, all of this applies to you as well. You need to become a Higher Self thinker to attract a similar soul. Like attracts like. Be what you would want your future mate to be. And the likelihood of your creating a Real Love in the future will be enhanced greatly.

- *I commit* to being faithful.
- *I commit* to being the best friend my mate could ever have.

Of course, none of us can honor our commitments all the time. Our ego (Lower Self) often gets in the way and pulls us away from love. The good news is that as we keep picking up the mirror and returning to the side of love once again, our commitments become easier and easier to honor.

"Susan, what if you honor your commitments and, horrors, your mate leaves the relationship?" Good question! One that I answered in *Embracing Uncertainty*:

> I joke that I always love my husband, Mark, to tell me he will love me forever, but I rest a little easier knowing I don't have to hold him to it! Forever was the theme of my first marriage. Obviously that didn't work. It didn't work for Mark's first marriage either. So what is the theme we've created for this marriage? We don't think about forever. We think about today. And, whenever we are together, we focus on how we can validate, respect, appreciate and care for one another. And what a wonderful love we have created. When you think a love will last forever, you tend to forget to focus on the now … and that is how love dies. When you focus on acting lovingly today, love tends to grow and grow. At least that's how it's been for us.[1]

You can see that having a Soul Mate right now does not guarantee a Soul Mate forever. We must enjoy the moment and never forget our highest priority: validating, respecting, appreciating and caring for one another. We must also live with the trust that … "Whatever happens, I'll handle it!" In this mental framework, the neediness disappears and the love can grow.

The road to Soul Mate status is clear, and the Love Lessons contained in this book will definitely send you in the right direction. Don't skim over them; they are important for you and your loved one. Study them. Live them. At the same time, have patience. I believe that living in the Lower Self, the most unloving part of who we are, is a bad habit. In order to break a bad habit, *constant repetition of the new, desired behavior is a must.* Again, I urge you to:

PRACTICE ... PRACTICE ... PRACTICE

The Journey is simple, but never-ending. Our ego is constantly getting in the way of love. We need to be ever-conscious of when it has taken control and move ourselves to the best of who we are: the Higher Self. In this way, little by little, our relationship is transformed. That's what Soul Mate training is all about.

We all can make the decision to live our lives with dignity, love and caring, and to push through the inner barriers that keep us from being a loving person. We all have that choice. It's about putting soul into everything you do. Trust me when I tell you that it feels so good to align with our Higher Self. Why would anyone resist? It is here that we finally understand that we have so much to give to our mate ... and to this world.

So commit! Right now commit to pushing through the fear and learning how to bring forward the loving and powerful energy of your Higher Self. As you live this way, moment by moment, day by day, in perfect time, you will find yourself moving closer and closer to real love, to finding your Soul Mate at last. Whatever it takes to get you to the place where happiness lies ... FEEL THE FEAR AND DO IT ANYWAY.

From my heart to yours,
Susan Jeffers

I will learn and grow from it all I will learn and grow from it all I will learn and grow from it all I will learn and grow from it all I will learn and grow from it all I will learn and grow from it all I will learn and grow from it all I will learn and grow from it all I will learn and grow from it all I will learn and grow from it all I will learn and grow from it all I will learn and grow from it all I will learn and grow from it all I will learn and grow from it all **I will learn and grow from it all** I will learn and grow from it all I will learn and grow from it all I will learn and grow from it all I will learn and grow from it all I will learn and grow from it all I will learn and grow from it all I will learn and grow from it all I will learn and grow from it all I will learn and grow from it all I will learn and grow from it all I will learn and grow from it all I will learn and grow from it all I will learn and grow from it all **I will learn and grow from it all** I will learn and grow from it all I will learn and grow from it all I will learn and grow from it all I will learn and grow from it all I will learn and grow from it all I will learn and grow from it all I will learn and grow from it all I will learn and grow from it all I will learn and grow from it all I will learn and grow from it all I will learn and grow from it all I will learn and grow from it all I will learn and grow from it all **I will learn and grow from it all** I will learn and grow from it all I will learn and grow from it all I will learn and grow from it all I will learn and grow from it all I will learn and grow from it all I will learn and grow from it all I will learn and grow from it all I will learn and grow from it all I will learn and grow from it all I will learn and grow from it all I will learn and grow from it all **I will learn and grow from it all** I

TAKE ANOTHER LOOK

There is no doubt that owning your magnificence is constantly to affim that you are a beautiful being and that your life matters ... and to act accordingly.

—SUSAN JEFFERS[1]

This isn't a book about ending a relationship, it's about creating a lasting love. But wherever there is love, there is the possibility of leaving, or being left. And I couldn't finish this book without offering a few suggestions if your relationship is not working out the way you had hoped it would.

Sometimes ending a relationship is necessary; but sometimes it is necessary to take another look. By picking up the mirror instead of the magnifying glass, it is possible that our upset with our mate can be transformed into a new form of connection and love. But if the relationship does ultimately end, remember that we can learn and grow from it all. (You're probably tired of hearing me say that, but it's such an important concept for you to keep in mind.) While breaking up is a painful experience, it is also an opportunity to learn what you need to work on within yourself in order to get it right the next time.

Many experts talk about unconditional love. Don't tell a soul, but between you and me, I really don't think that such a thing as unconditional love exists between mere mortals. At least, I haven't seen any evidence of it. (I guess the closest we come to unconditional love has to do with our children, but even there, we are constantly being tested!) Nor do I believe that love *should* be unconditional:

I believe that love between two adults needs to be earned.

And what sometimes looks like unconditional love is often a bad case of neediness, which causes us to hang on to someone we really would be better off letting go of. "But I really love him/her!" often means, "I really need him/her!"

I believe that the most anyone can ask is that we see the light within them that perhaps has been dimmed by difficult life experiences. And maybe that is one way of defining unconditional love—seeing the light no matter what the behavior. But *seeing the light within doesn't necessarily mean that we should stay in a hurtful relationship.* "I love you and I'm leaving" is about as unconditional as a very hurtful love should get.

I also believe it is important to let go of unrealistic or unreasonable expectations, but there are some expectations that are truly justified in a relationship, for example, the expectation that we are treated with honor, respect and a sense of caring. Sometimes these basic attributes of love are not forthcoming from our partner and we have to think again about whether we want to be in the relationship or not.

It is important to understand that there are reasons for honoring ourselves by having an "out the door" policy when it comes to the behavior of our mate. The folowing are three obvious examples:

Physical abuse: This is a "first time, shame on you; second time, shame on me" situation. If I was physically abused by my mate, I would be out the door so fast, I would leave a cloud of dust behind me. Of this, I am sure. Leaving is not something to hesitate about in such a situation. By the way, this goes for abused men as well. We think of physical abuse as perpetrated only by men. While it is true that more physical abuse is perpetrated by men, some women also physically abuse men.

Whether you are a man or a woman, if your mate is physically abusive, I suggest you leave and shut the door behind you. If you are too frightened to leave because of threats from your mate, or if you believe you "deserve" the beatings, or if you don't think you can make it on your own, please seek outside help. Don't let shame stop you; there is nothing to be ashamed of. It is your mate's behavior that is the problem, not yours. Certainly physical abuse is the best reason I know of to end a relationship.

Verbal abuse: Extreme verbal abuse is a no-no as well. All of us have been insulting and insulted every now and then when anger is in control, but I am talking about constant verbal abuse that berates, embarrasses and tries to make us feel less than we are. There is no reason for any man or woman to put up with this kind of abuse.

If your mate agrees to seek help, a reprieve could be had for a short period of time (whereas where there is physical violence, I recommend no reprieve), but no one deserves to live with a person who constantly curses, screams or berates him/her in any way. Anger management courses for your mate or group and individual therapy for both of you sometimes can help. It is very hard to live with the disdain we feel coming from our mate when he/she treats us so badly. That's not what love is all about.

Addiction to alcohol or drugs: A young man in one of my workshops talked to me after class about his girlfriend:

235

"I love her, but she drinks too much. She won't go for help because she doesn't even see that she has a problem. I know I'm supposed to be supportive, but if I go along with her drinking, I don't think this is helping her at all." I agreed. He said he has become a nag about her drinking, but he doesn't know what else to do. I asked him if he was willing to accept her exactly as she is—an active alcoholic. He—wisely, in my opinion—said, "No." I explained that there really is nothing he can do to change her behavior. She has to want to change it herself. I suggested that he just say, "I love you, but I can no longer be in this relationship." And to move on. He agreed he had no choice, and he moved out the following week.

As hard as it is to break up a relationship, it is far more difficult to maintain it when one partner refuses to take responsibility for his or her own destructive behavior. This doesn't mean that there aren't couples in long-term relationships where one of the partners is an alcoholic or drug addict, but it is obvious that these are not happy relationships. Living with an alcoholic or drug addict is very difficult, indeed. If you are living with an addict who is not acknowledging that he/she has a problem, leaving the relationship is justified. Many have found a great deal of help at Al-Anon, which is an adjunct AA program for the family and friends of alcoholics.[2]

On a more positive note, if your mate realizes that he/she has an addiction problem and goes for help, the chances are very good that the relationship can survive. I've seen it happen often. Many men and women who are recovering alcoholics or recovering drug addicts are proving to be loving mates.

Yes, there is always a chance that they will return to alcohol or drugs, but very often they become more spiritual, loving and responsible human beings, especially if they follow the teachings of a spiritual program such as that of AA. I know a number of recovering alcoholics who have not only stopped drinking, but who have also realized their value in this world and are doing beautiful things. Their relationships thrive.

For good reasons, any one of these three no-no's justifiably signals that we need to end the relationship. And you may be able to come up with a few more no-no's of your own. But most relationships do not end for such obvious reasons. In fact, sometimes we don't even understand why relationships end, which is why I recommend that before you decide to end such a relationship, you take another look. This means: You pick up the mirror instead of the magnifying glass and learn as much as you can about what you need to change within yourself. Remember, if you don't learn from this relationship, you most likely will make the same mistakes the next time around.

Here are some examples of "take another look" situations in which great learning is possible:

The fantasy ends. "Some enchanted evening" strikes again. Very often we marry a fantasy instead of a person. As might be predicted, one day reality sets in, and our prince or princess turns into an ordinary human being with human limitations and frailties. Our unrealistic, and sometimes unfair, expectations blind us to the beauty that is there and we want to leave the relationship. But before leaving, it is important to *take another look.*

We want to "find ourselves." Sometimes we marry too early, never having had a chance to be on our own. Unhealthy dependencies result and we decide to leave in order to "find ourselves." We have to ask ourselves, "Is it really necessary for me to leave in order for me to find myself?" Maybe yes; maybe no. But before leaving, it is important to *take another look.*

Our "dreams" are unacceptable to the other. I do believe we have to honor our dreams—our hopes for the future. If our mate can't accept what we want to do in life, we understandably may choose to leave. Earlier I used the example of a woman wanting to be out in the workforce and her husband wanting her to stay at home. If our mate can't accept our dreams because of his/her own fears, expectations or need for control, we certainly would be wise to leave. Stifling our dreams is stifling our soul—our purpose. I don't think any person could have stopped me from pursuing my dream, nor would I attempt to stop anyone else from pursuing theirs. We have to ask ourselves, "Is it necessary to leave in order to live my dreams?" Again, maybe yes; maybe no. But before leaving, it is important to *take another look.*

The "contract" changes. "You were what I wanted when I met you; now I want something different." Sometimes the people we choose are meant for a certain period of our lives and not for another. We grow, and often we grow apart. We change, develop different interests, and sometimes incompatibility is the result. Perhaps there comes a tipping point where it is impossible to find our way back to each other again. But before leaving, it is important to *take another look.*

Our mate's insecurity pulls us down. It often happens that when one partner begins to grow, the other feels insecure and pulls him/her down. If we do all we can to assure our partner of our love and he/she continues to pull us down, we need to get away from that kind of negative energy. It is demoralizing. If all else fails, leaving may be the best thing to do. But before leaving, it is important to *take another look.*

We focus too much on externals. If our mate has not lived up to our expectations in terms of looks, money and the like, I think we need to raise our standards. By this I mean that we need to focus on the heart and soul of our mate instead of the externals. Is he/she a loving, caring person? We ultimately may decide to leave. But before leaving, it is important to *take another look.*

Our trust is gone. If we discover our mate has been unfaithful, it is very hard to regain our trust in the relationship (as you learned in Chapter 9). Our disappointment is understandable and it is very tempting to leave. It is hard to live with someone you no longer trust. Yet it often happens that a couple can pull it together even after one or both of the partners has strayed. I've seen it happen. So before leaving, it is important to *take another look.*

We've taken another look! Yes, the time to leave comes for many of us when we have worked on ourselves, tried our very best to change what doesn't work, and communicated our upset to our mate. One morning we wake up and know deep within our heart that the relationship is over. Perhaps our partner continues to treat us in a less than loving way. Perhaps what he/she does is simply not okay with us. Perhaps, for whatever reason, it is simply over. In such a case, we've probably taken as many looks as we need to. And it is truly clear to us that it is time to say goodbye. *No more looks required!*

The above situations offer a wonderful opportunity to practice becoming more powerful and loving within ourselves, to determine where our expectations are unreasonable, to learn how to appreciate the good that is there, and to get creative in terms of fixing the problem at hand.

It is important to realize that the only way to learn how to be in a relationship is to *be in* a relationship! As I mentioned earlier, between my marriages, I had a habit of leaving relationships when trouble arose. My thinking was that I hadn't yet learned enough to be in a relationship. It finally occurred to me that, while I functioned beautifully on my own, *if I wanted to learn how to be in a relationship, I had to be in a relationship!* (It's amazing how the obvious often eludes us.)

In the beginning, before Mark and I got married, there were times when I wanted to leave him, as I left all the others. But this time I was determined not to run, but to learn. And I learned so much—particularly that it was my own fears, my own insecurities that were creating most of the problems. As I worked on becoming a more confident person within the relationship, as I learned how to become "safely vulnerable," as I learned the secret of honest communication, it all fell into place and our love thrived. In the process, I was able to focus on what was really wonderful about Mark … and there is so much that is wonderful about him.

Your relationship may or may not work out after a certain period of time. One thing I can guarantee is that if you do everything you can to work it out before leaving, you will rest easier. Dorothy offers a perfect example. For two years after she separated, she and her ex-husband did many things to see if they could work it out: vacations together, individual therapy, group therapy and so on. Then one day she woke up and just "knew" her marriage was truly over. Because she had made every effort to resolve the differences between herself and her husband, she never looked back and wondered if she had made a mistake. She knew it simply would not work out between them as man and wife. Thankfully, she and her ex are very good friends today. You see, even so-called unhappy endings can transform into a new kind of bond that is very beautiful indeed. In that, it was a happy ending after all.

By the way, if you ultimately decide to leave, don't punish yourself by thinking you chose the wrong partner. For various reasons, your partner was right at a certain time in your life. I know my first marriage wasn't wrong. It was absolutely right for the time. It was my vehicle for learning many things about myself and about life itself. There are no guarantees. As we learn and grow from our experiences, we realize that, even if the relationship ends, our lives have been enriched in so many ways. In that, "It's all happening perfectly."

"Susan, but what if my mate leaves?" Good question. Yes, it can be the biggest shock of our lives if our mate informs us that he/she is leaving. This can be a fierce blow to the heart for both men and women. It is really critical for all concerned to understand that, after an initial period of mourning our loss, we will get to the other side of the pain. When the heart opens it is vulnerable. It can get wounded so easily. But when we know we will always get to the other side, we can be "safely vulnerable," knowing we can handle it all.

It is important to reject the victim mentality and—one step at a time—take responsibility for creating a new and fulfilling life for yourself. Make "Happiness is the best revenge" your motto. With this thought ever-present in your mind, work to increase your self-esteem (which is often deflated when our mate leaves), and find new adventures, new experiences and ultimately a new sense of joy. You have to learn how to let go, to forgive and move forward, looking back only to learn. In this way, you can build a beautiful life for yourself.

Let me reiterate, you have to remember that even though your partner left, the relationship was not a waste. As you focus on the learning, you have a much better chance of getting it right the next time. For this reason, I consider all relationships, even the worst of them, good in that they give us an opportunity to grow.

A word of advice: Many signs of pulling apart from your partner appear long before they become a visible problem. It's important not to let things slide too far down the slippery slope of discontent. Be very conscious, and if you see a problem emerging, tackle it in the beginning. Early help can save many a relationship.

Whether we leave a relationship or are left, a period of upset is only natural. How could you share a life with a person and not feel a hole in your life and in your heart when the relationship ends? But as you set about creating a rich, whole, beautiful life for yourself, the hole in your heart and in your life is quickly filled. Remember, there isn't only one drink of water in the proverbial desert. Once a relationship ends, there are many opportunities to find love again. And always remember that the more loving you become, the easier it will be to find someone to love.

LOVE LESSONS

1) **Again ... no blame:** If the relationship ends, it is tempting to blame our mate for all that went wrong—or, just as bad, to blame ourselves. In America, we have so-called "no-fault" divorces. I like that. We got together, it didn't work out and we are now ending it. If we can restrain ourselves from blaming our mate, we can open our hearts to their humanness, knowing we are all doing the best we can; we can look inside and see what we can improve within ourselves to make it better the next time around. Trust me when I tell you, until you stop the blame, you won't be ready for a healthy relationship.

2) **Learn the secret of being attractive to members of the opposite sex.** Mark and I had an illuminating experience the other night. We were at a large dinner party, happy to be sitting next to a lovely woman who was vibrant and seemingly very likeable. As the evening progressed, she told us she was recently divorced. As she began speaking about her ex-husband, a transformation took place. Her anger was unleashed and this very beautiful woman turned ugly right before our eyes! Her venom made us want to move to another table!

It is so important for many reasons that you deal with your anger. Your anger is your clue that you are refusing to take responsibility for your choices in life. In this woman's case, she surely wasn't taking responsibility for any of the choices she had made! Trust me when I tell you that you cannot be attractive to an emotionally healthy member of the opposite sex if your anger dims the love within you. So learn all the techniques for dealing with anger within the pages of this and my other books, particularly *Opening Our Hearts to Men* (yes, it's great for you men as well.) You'll be healthier, happier and much more attractive!

Remember, even if your mate leaves, even if your mate has hurt you deeply, even if you decide to leave an unhappy situation:

YOU, AND ONLY YOU, ARE IN CONTROL OF YOUR REACTIONS TO ALL THAT HAPPENS TO YOU IN LIFE. REACT IN A WAY THAT GIVES YOU POWER, PEACE OF MIND AND LOVE ... ALL OF WHICH MAKE YOU BEAUTIFUL AS A HUMAN BEING.

3) *Learn how to forgive.* Forgiveness is essential if a relationship ends. It may take a little while, but the sooner we forgive, the better for our happiness and even for our health. In *Feel the Fear and Do It Anyway,* I presented an exercise that I find very effective in helping us to forgive. It goes like this:

Find an empty room and turn off the telephone. Put on some soothing music. Sit down in a comfortable chair and close your eyes. Visualize someone who brings up a lot of anger or pain in you. Picture them in front of you. First, surround them with rays of healing white light and tell them that you wish them all good things—everything they could possibly want in their lifetime. Thank them for whatever they have given you. Keep doing this until you feel your negative emotions leaving.[3]

Trust me when I tell you that this is not easy, but I think you already know that. In fact, you may be wanting to throw this book at me! If your experience doing this exercise is anything like mine, you will find yourself going through rage, tears and anger. "Wish him/her good things? No way! I want him/her to suffer!" But as you continue repeating this exercise over a number of days, you will be amazed to find yourself reaching the point where you truly can forgive. You come to the realization that we are all just doing the best we can relative to who we are as human beings.

It is so important to drop the anger and forgive so that you can move into future relationships without carrying the heavy baggage of past relationships. To forgive is also a very necessary step in fulfilling our Higher Purpose, that of becoming a more loving person.

4) ***Get help.*** When things are truly difficult, therapy is always an option. Understand that there are good therapists and bad therapists. A bad therapist may mean well, but he or she may be operating from ideas that do not support the best of who you are. My idea of a good therapist is one who does not make you a victim of your mate or anyone or anything else, but rather makes you feel you are a strong human being who is capable of making appropriate changes in your life. Any therapist who encourages you to blame instead of taking responsibility for your life is not one I would recommend you go to. Sometimes therapists increase anger instead of healing your heart. I've often seen it happen.

The truth is that we are NOT helpless victims at the mercy of external circumstances. We are all capable of creating powerful and loving solutions to all the problems in our lives. A therapist who helps us to recognize our own inner power is a wonderful therapist indeed.

5) ***Write yourself a reminder letter.*** If you are clear that your relationship is not going to work out, write yourself a long letter about why you want it to end. Detail the feelings you had when you were hurt in any way. I did this before leaving my first marriage, and whenever loneliness or fear took over after I left, I picked up the letter to remind myself why I left in the first place. It truly was a great reminder and gave me strength to create a new life. I have suggested this idea to a number of people who have found it very effective.

Remember that just as we can learn from a relationship, we can also learn from the break-up of a relationship. Your unhappiness after a break-up doesn't mean you should be back in the relationship. It only means that there is a hole in your heart that needs filling. It is time to fill your life with many things that make you feel good about yourself. You can't think of anything to do? I'll give you a suggestion. Just look around. There are so many things that need to be done to make this a better world. Start there. As you begin to help this world in your own way, eventually you will begin to feel whole. The neediness disappears, and life is good. It's a powerful place to be and puts you in a much better position to create a beautiful new love. Onward!

ENDNOTES

Please note that the resources mentioned below may not be available when you seek them. It's not always possible to know what is in or out of print. Not to worry! The world works in wonderful ways. If one thing is not available, you always will find something else to help you on your journey to lasting love.

Chapter 1

1. Hooks, Bell. *All About Love: New Visions.* William Morrow, 2000, p. 4.

2. www.beccascloset.org Becca (Rebecca Kirtman) was a wonderful 16-year- old who cared about those who were less fortunate than she was. She started Becca's Closet by single-handedly collecting 250 prom dresses allowing many young women to attend their prom in style. Tragically, she was killed in an automobile accident on August 20, 2003. Those who loved her expanded on her dreams and have, among other things, created a college scholarship fund for those who need a helping hand.

3. Music and lyrics by Stephen Sondheim, book by James Lapine.

4. McGraw, Dr. Phillip. "Dr. Phil: The Love Survey." In *O (The Oprah Magazine)*, February, 2004, p. 32.

5. Johnson, Robert A. *We: Understanding the Psychology of Romantic Love.* Harper and Row, San Francisco, 1983, p. 195.

Chapter 2

1. Wilde, Stuart. *Miracles.* Wisdom Books, Inc., Taos, New Mexico, 1983, p. 6.

2. Jeffers, Susan. *Feel the Fear And Do It Anyway.* Fawcett Columbine, New York, 1987, pp. 15-16.

3. Jeffers, Susan and Gradstein, Donna. *I Can Handle It: How to Have a Confident Child.* Vermillion Books (Random House), London, 2002.

4. Richo, David. *How To Be An Adult in Relationships: The Five Keys to Mindful Loving.* Shambhala Publications, Inc., Boston, Massachusetts (Distributed in the U.S. by Random House, Inc.), 2002, p. 155.

5. You can read or listen to *THE FEAR-LESS SERIES: Inner Talk for A Confident Day, Inner Talk for A Love that Works, Inner Talk for Peace of Mind.* Hodder and Stoughton, London, 1997.

Chapter 3

1. Grayson, Henry. *Mindful Loving: 10 Practices for Creating Deeper Connections.* Gotham Books (Penguin Group), New York, 2003, p. 7.

2. Ibid., p. 66.

Chapter 4

1. Welwood, John. *Toward a Psychology of Awakening: Buddhism, Psychotherapy, and the Path of Personal and Spiritual Transformation.* Shambhala Publications, Inc., Boston & London, 2002, pp. 48-49.

Chapter 5

1. Viscott, David. *How To Live with Another Person.* Arbor House, New York, 1974, pp. 103-104.

2. Keyes, Jr., Ken, *How to Enjoy Your Life in Spite of it All.* Living Love Publications, St. Mary, Kentucky, 1980, p. 5.

3. For a much expanded explanation of this exercise, the "Grid of Life," go to *Feel the Fear and Do It Anyway* and/or *Feel the Fear and Beyond.*

Chapter 6

1. Shain, Merle. *Hearts That We Broke Long Ago.* Bantam Books, New York, 1983, pp. 81-82.

2. The address of the publisher of this very creative spoof was Newport House, 100 Via Estrada, Suite P, Laguna Hills, CA 92653.

3. Levy, Alison Rose. "Each Other's Stuff" in *Spirituality and Health*, Fall issue, 2000 http://www.spiritualityhealth.com/ newsh/items/article/item 51.html.

4. Carnegie, Dale. *How To Win Friends And Influence People.* Pocket Books, New York, 1936, p. 66.

5. Erhard, Werner. *Celebrating Your Relationships.* (audiotape), Soundworks, 1985.

6. Jeffers, Susan. *Opening Our Hearts to Men: Taking Charge of Our Lives and Creating a Love that Works.* Fawcett Columbine, New York, 1989, Chapter 8 (The Man Behind the Mask).

7. Jeffers, Susan. *Dare to Connect: Reaching Out in Romance, Friendship and the Workplace.* Judy Piatkus (Publishers), Ltd., London, 1992, Chapter 8 (Sharing the Deepest, the Darkest and the Dirtiest).

Chapter 7

1. Williamson, Marianne. *Cosmic Adulthood.* (audiotape), 1987. A lecture based on The Course in Miracles.

2. Keyes, Jr., Ken. *A Conscious Person's Guide to Relationship.* Living Love Publications, Kentucky, 1979, p.11.

Chapter 8

1. These telling words of Nora Ephron are quoted by author Susan Maushart in *The Mask of Motherhood.* Random House Australia Pty Ltd, NSW Australia, 1997, p. 101.

2. Jeffers, Susan. *I'm Okay ... You're a Brat: Setting the Priorities Straight and Freeing You from the Guilt and Mad Myths of Parenthood.* Renaissance Books, 1999, p. 74.

3. Clinton, Hillary. *It Takes a Village.* Simon and Schuster, New York, 1996.

4. To learn more about a child's "Circle of Being," go to *I'm Okay ... You're a Brat,* Chapter 5.

Chapter 9

1. Jeffers, Susan. *Opening Our Hearts to Men: Taking Charge of Our Lives and Creating a Love that Works.* Fawcett Columbine, New York, 1989, p. 189.

Chapter 10

1. Sherven, Judith & Sniechowski, James. *The New Intimacy: Discovering the Magic at the Heart of Your Differences.* Health Communications, Inc., 1997, p. 140.

2. Weiner-Davis, Michele. *The Sex-Starved Marriage: A Couple's Guide to Boosting Their Marriage Libido.* Simon & Schuster, 2003, p. 8.

3. Deane, Geoff. "Life After Birth: When One and One Makes Three," *Arena Magazine,* Spring, 1994, p. 56.

4. Jeffers, Susan. *I'm Okay ... You're a Brat: Setting the Priorities Straight and Freeing You from the Guilt and Mad Myths of Parenthood.* Renaissance Books, 1999, pp. 78-79.

5. Ibid., p. 79.

6. Ibid., p. 80.

7. Brewer, Sarah: *Intimate Relations: Living and Loving in Later Life.* Age Concern, Age Concern Books, England, 2004.

8. Margolis, Jonathan. "The Rise of the 21st Century Mrs. Robinson" in the *Sunday Times Magazine,* June 6, 2004, p. 33.

9. Moseley, Douglas & Moseley, Naomi. *The Shadow Side of Intimate Relationships:What's Going On Between the Scenes.* North Star Publications, Massachusetts, 2000, p. 224.

10. Joy and Shana's sex shop is called The Rubber Tree and it is located at 5018 E. 2nd. St., Long Beach, California 90803.

Chapter 11

1. Johnson, Robert A. *We: Understanding the Psychology of Romantic Love.* Harper & Row, San Francisco, 1983, p. 201.

2. Markman, Howard, Stanley, Scott M., & Blumberg, Susan L. *Fighting for Your Relationship.* Jossey-Bass (a Wiley company), San Francisco, 2001, p. 27.

3. McGraw, Dr. Phillip. "Dr. Phil: The Love Survey." In *O* (*The Oprah Magazine*), February, 2004, p.32.

4. Carnegie, Dale. *How To Win Friends And Influence People.* Pocket Books, New York, 1936, p. 231.

5. Ibid., p. 237.

6. Shedd, Charlie & Martha. *How to Stay in Love.* Ace Books, New York, 1981, p. 13.

Chapter 12

1. John Welwood. *Toward a Psychology of Awakening: Buddhism, Psychotherapy, and the Path of Personal and Spiritual Transformation.* Shambala Publications, Inc., (Boston and London), 2002, p. 234.

2. Jeffers, Susan. *Opening Our Hearts to Men: Taking Charge of Our Lives and Creating a Love that Works.* Fawcett Columbine, New York, 1989, p. 95.

3. Elliott, John. "Men Want to Wed ... Women Want to Roam." *The Sunday Times,* March 21, 2004, p. 10 (news section).

Chapter 13

1. Williamson, Marianne, *All I Give Is Given to Myself.* (audiotape) A lecture based on The Course in Miracles, 1987.

2. To read (and hear) this horrifying recipe in its entirety, go to http://www.abc.net.au/queensland/federation/stories/s2246 72.htm.

3. In "True Feminists Only Want Equality," by Keira Wagner. (www.ryunlv.com) Go to Archives, Monday, September 16, 2002.

4. Williamson, Marianne. *"Intensive: Men and Women #2"* (audiotape) A lecture based on The Course in Miracles, 1987.

Conclusion

1. Jeffers, Susan. *Embracing Uncertainty: Achieving Peace of Mind As We Face the Unknown.* St. Martin's Press, New York, 2002, p. 54.

Addendum

1. Jeffers, Susan. *Opening Our Hearts to Men: Taking Charge of Our Lives and Creating a Love that Works.* Fawcett Columbine, New York, 1989, p. 234.

2. To learn more about Al-Anon, log onto http://www.alanon.alateen.org/about.html. Al-Anon meetings are held in 115 countries. Meetings are also available on-line.

3. Jeffers, Susan. *Feel the Fear and Do It Anyway.* Fawcett Columbine, New York, 1987, p. 176.

ABOUT THE AUTHOR

Susan Jeffers, Ph.D., recently dubbed the Queen of Self-Help, is the internationally renowned author of many books including the best-selling *Feel the Fear and Do It Anyway, End the Struggle and Dance with Life, Life is Huge!,* and the award winning *Embracing Uncertainty.* Her books, which have been published in over 100 countries and translated into 36 languages, have helped millions of people overcome their fear, heal their relationships and move forward in life. She is a well-known public speaker and media personality. Susan lives with her husband in Los Angeles. Her popular website is www.susanjeffers.com.